$3.50

Reading from the Beginning
The Shaping of the Hebrew Psalter

וַאֲנִי קִרֲבַת אֱלֹהִים לִי־טוֹב
(Psalm 73:28)

Reading from the Beginning

The Shaping of the Hebrew Psalter

by
Nancy L. deClaissé-Walford

MERCER UNIVERSITY PRESS
1997

ISBN 0-86554-567-7 MUP/H439

📖

The paper used in this publication meets the minimum requirements
of American National Standard for Information Sciences—
Permanence of Paper for Printed Library Materials, ANSI Z39.48-1984.

📖

Library of Congress Cataloging-in-Publication Data

deClaissé-Walford, Nancy L., 1954–   .
   Reading from the beginning :
the shaping of the Hebrew Psalter /
   by Nancy L. deClaissé-Walford.
      ix+143pp. 6x9" (15x23cm.)
Includes bibliographical references and indexes.
         ISBN 0-86554-567-7
   1. Bible. O.T. Psalms—Criticism, redaction.
         BS1430.2 .D38   1997
         223'.206—dc21   97-41067
                                          CIP

Contents

Preface

This study of the Hebrew Psalter approaches the text as a story within a canonical context. I began with the question, "Why these 150 psalms and why in this order?" and found answers in the hermeneutical underpinnings—the footprints—of the text's shaping community. The community shaped the text into its present form because within that form, and not some other, it found answers to basic existential questions, such as "Who are we?" and "What are we to do in our present circumstances?" The canonical Psalter attained its final shape in the postexilic period of ancient Israel's history, and its story is the product of the exigencies of postexilic life. In order to fully understand the Psalter, we must understand something about the life circumstances of the shaping community. With the benefit of that understanding, readers and hearers can then appropriate the story to the exigencies of their own lives and their own questions of identity. The affirmation of the story in the Psalter was central to the survival and future of the postexilic ancient Israelite community and remains central to the survival and future of the believing community today.

My methodology is canonical. I became interested in the canonical method of biblical scholarship after reading James Sanders's essay, "Adaptable for Life: The Nature and Function of Canon,"[1] in which he argues that a text becomes authoritative within a community, not because some person or authority decrees that that text should be authoritative, but because the community finds value in the text. Sanders wrote that

> certain traditions in ancient Israel bore repeating. . . . Such material, which met a need in one situation, was apparently able to meet another need in another situation. And that is precisely the kind of tradition that

---

[1]James A. Sanders, "Adaptable for Life: The Nature and Function of Canon," in *From Sacred Story to Sacred Text* (Philadelphia: Fortress Press, 1987) 9-39.

becomes canonical—material that bears repeating in a later moment both because of the need of the later moment and because of the value or power of the material repeated (the dialogue between them).[2]

The canonical approach to the text of the Hebrew Bible focuses questions about canon and authority away from questions about oral forms, authors, and redactors and toward the proper subject of study—the shaping community.

The title for the book, *Reading from the Beginning*, is taken from a dialogue between the White Rabbit and the King of Hearts in Lewis Carroll's *Alice in Wonderland*. Paul W. Gaebelein, Jr., who taught Hebrew, Akkadian, and Archaeology of the Bible at Fuller Theological Seminary in Pasadena, California, used the wise words of the King of Hearts when students asked him questions such as how many pages term papers for his classes were to contain or how many hours of study they should devote to a particular topic. He replied, "Begin at the beginning. Go on until you come to the end. And then stop." When one approaches the Hebrew scriptures canonically, then the words are apt indeed. Frederic W. Bush, also of Fuller Theological Seminary, patiently taught me Semitic languages and instigated my lifelong passion for the Hebrew language. W. H. Bellinger, Jr., of Baylor University, introduced me to the study of the Hebrew Psalter and persistently encouraged my research work. The Book of Psalms Section of the Society of Biblical Literature graciously allowed me to present and "test" my ideas concerning the shaping of the Psalter. R. Alan Culpepper, of the McAfee School of Theology at Mercer University, provided a faculty environment that allowed me to bring this project to completion. And Mercer University Press believed enough in the value of my work to chance its publication. To each of them, I owe an immeasurable debt of gratitude.

To my husband Steve, and my sons Calvin and Aaron, I owe the greatest debt. Without their love, their encouragement, and their daily solid grounding in reality, I am sure this project would not have come to fruition.

(Psalm 73:28) וַאֲנִי קִרֲבַת אֱלֹהִים לִי־טוֹב

Atlanta, 7 August 1997   *Nancy L. deClaissé-Walford*

---

[2]Ibid., 21.

Abbreviations

AB	Anchor Bible
ANET	Pritchard, *Ancient Near Eastern Texts Relating to the O.T.*
BHS	*Biblia Hebraica Stuttgartensia*
CBQ	*Catholic Biblical Quarterly*
EVV	English versions (especially regarding versification)
FAT	Forschungen zum Alten Testament
FBBS	Facet Books, Biblical Series
GBS	Guides to Biblical Scholarship
HBT	*Horizons in Biblical Theology*
HS	*Hebrew Studies*
HUCA	Hebrew Union College Annual
JBL	*Journal of Biblical Literature*
JSPSSup	Journal for the Study of the Pseudepigrapha supplement series
JSOT	*Journal for the Study of the Old Testament*
JSOTSup	JSOT supplement series
JSS	*Journal of Semitic Studies*
JTS	*Journal of Theological Studies*
MT	Masoretic Text
NCB	New Century Bible
NEchtB	Die neue Echter Bibel. Kommentar zum Alten Testament mit de Einheitsübersetzung
SBLDS	Society of Biblical Literature dissertation series
STDJ	Studies on the Texts of the Desert of Judah
VT	*Vetus Testamentum*
WBC	Word Biblical Commentary
ZAW	*Zeitschrift für die alttestamentliche Wissenschaft*

Chapter 1

Introduction
and the Canonical Method

Introduction

Beginning at the Beginning

[The White Rabbit has just found an important piece of evidence.]
"What's in it?" said the Queen.

"I haven't opened it yet," said the White Rabbit; "but it seems to be a letter, written . . . to somebody."

"It must have been that," said the King, "unless it was written to nobody, which isn't usual, you know."

"Who is it directed to?" said one of the jurymen.

"It isn't directed at all," said the White Rabbit; "in fact, there's nothing written on the *outside*." He unfolded the paper as he spoke, and added, "It isn't a letter after all: it's a set of verses." . . .

"Read them," said the King.

The White Rabbit put on his spectacles. "Where shall I begin, please your majesty?" he asked.

"Begin at the beginning," the King said, very gravely, "and go on till you come to the end: then stop."[1]

This is not bad advice from a slightly befuddled fairy-tale king. How often have biblical scholars posed the White Rabbit's question and, in their eagerness to dissect and study the texts, not heeded the King's advice? If we approach the Hebrew Bible as we approach other works of

---

[1]Lewis Carroll, *Alice in Wonderland*, 2nd ed., A Norton Critical Edition, ed. Donald J. Gray (New York: W. W. Norton, 1992) 94.

literature, then the beginning seems a very good place to begin. And if we try to describe the canonical process[2] by which a book or books of the Hebrew Bible arrived at their present shape, then the King's words are appropriate indeed. "Begin at the beginning. . . ."

"It isn't a letter after all: it's a set of verses." Can we apply the principle, though, to those portions of the Hebrew Bible that are not really "story" but are "collections" of material? I think we can. Present-day study of the Book of Psalms has moved in a "begin at the beginning" direction. Brevard Childs encourages scholars to go beyond a historical-critical analysis of texts and to take seriously their canonical shapes.[3] In *The Editing of the Hebrew Psalter*, Gerald Wilson convincingly demonstrates that the Psalter evidences purposeful editing and that it told a "story" to the ancient Israelites—a story about their past history, their present situation, and their hope for the future.[4] J. Clinton McCann, Jr., in *The Shape and Shaping of the Psalter*, observes that scholars are increasingly aware that "the purposeful placement of psalms within the collection seems to have given the final form of the whole Psalter a function and message greater than the sum of its parts."[5] In *A Theological Introduction to the Book of Psalms*, he urges readers to "take seriously the canonical shape of the Psalter, . . . and begin at the beginning."[6] We have certainly moved beyond the form-critical and cult-functional approaches to the Psalter which Hermann Gunkel, Sigmund Mowinckel, and Claus Westermann originated.[7] These methods largely ignore the

---

[2]James A. Sanders defines canonical process in an essay entitled "Canonical Context and Canonical Criticism," in *From Sacred Story to Sacred Text* (Philadelphia: Fortress Press, 1987) 164.

[3]Brevard S. Childs, *Introduction to the Old Testament as Scripture* (Philadelphia: Fortress Press, 1979).

[4]See Gerald H. Wilson, *The Editing of the Hebrew Psalter*, SBLDS 76 (Chico CA.: Scholars Press, 1985).

[5]J. Clinton McCann, Jr., ed., *The Shape and Shaping of the Psalter*, JSOTSup 159 (Sheffield UK: JSOT Press, 1993) 7.

[6]J. Clinton McCann, Jr., *A Theological Introduction to the Book of Psalms: The Psalms as Torah* (Nashville: Abingdon Press, 1993) 25.

[7]In additional to the works cited above, see, for example, the recent works of Matthias Millard, *Die Komposition des Psalters: ein formgeschichlichter Ansatz*, FAT 9 (Tübingen: J. C. B. Mohr, 1994); Erhard S. Gerstenberger, "Der Psalter als Buch und als Sammlung," in *Neue Wege der Psalmenforschung: für*

canonical order of the psalms and analyze them instead by type and original *Sitz im Leben.*

This study asks: "Why these 150 psalms and why in the particular order in which we find them in the Psalter? How did the postexilic Israelite community shape the book we call the Psalter? What were the hermeneutical underpinnings of the process that resulted in the five-book, 150-psalm arrangement of the work?" I am not the first to ask the questions. The Midrash on Psalm 3 states:

> As to the exact order of David's Psalms, Scripture says elsewhere: *Man knoweth not the order thereof* (Job 28:13). R. Eleazar taught: The sections of Scripture are not arranged in their proper order. For if they were arranged in their proper order, and any man so read them, he would be able to resurrect the dead and perform other miracles. For this reason the proper order of the sections of Scripture is hidden from mortals and is known only to the Holy One, blessed be He, who said, *"Who, as I, can read and declare it, and set it in order?"* (Isa 44:7).
>
> When R. Joshua ben Levi sought to arrange the Psalms in their proper order, a heavenly voice came forth and commanded: "Do not rouse that which slumbers!"[8]

Perhaps Rabbi ben Levi is wiser than I, but I maintain that we can discover the hermeneutical "logic" for the arrangement of the psalms within the Psalter. Today we have only the final, canonical shape of the Psalter with which to work. But from that final "shape," we can move to the underlying "shaping"—the process by which the book achieved its canonical form.

Walter Beyerlin, 3-13, ed. Klaus Seybold and Erich Zenger (Freiburg/New York: Herder, 1994); Terrence Collins, "Decoding the Psalms: A Structural Approach to the Psalter," JSOT 37 (1987): 41-60; Frank-Lothar Hossfeld and Erich Zenger, *Die Psalmen I, Psalm 1 - 50*, NEchtB (Würzburg: Echter Verlag, 1993); Klaus Koch, "Der Psalter und seine Redaktionsgeschichte," in *Neue Wege der Psalmenforschung*, 243-77; James L. Mays, *The Lord Reigns: A Theological Handbook to the Psalms* (Louisville: Westminster/John Knox Press, 1994) 117-45; and J. Clinton McCann, Jr., "The Book of Pslams," in *The New Interpreter's Bible*, vol. 4, ed. Leander E. Keck et al. (Nashville: Abingdon Press, 1996) 643-66.

[8]William G. Braude, *The Midrash on Psalms*, vol. 1 (New Haven CT: Yale University Press, 1959) 49-50. Braude writes that while the Midrash on the Psalter was compiled beginning in the second century CE, much of the material included in it dates to well before the common era.

When the ancient Israelites returned from exile in the late sixth century, their Persian overseers allowed them to rebuild their temple and reestablish their cult. Temple and cult were restored, but the nation-state which the Davidic dynasty had ruled was not. Except for a brief time of independence during the second and first centuries BCE, the people lived continuously as vassals, first to the Persians, then to the Greeks, and then to the Romans, throughout the period of the second temple. Gone forever were the days of King David and the nation of YHWH which stretched "from Dan to Beersheba."

Under the same circumstances, many nation-states in the ancient Near East simply disappeared from history. But ancient Israel did not. The postexilic community found a new structure for existence and identity which went beyond traditional concepts of nationhood. Temple and cult, rather than king and court, now had to be the center of life. How would the community achieve a new viewpoint, a new mindset? Donn F. Morgan, in *Between Text and Community: The "Writings" in Canonical Interpretation*, asserts that understanding this new mindset is a fundamental key to understanding postexilic Israel. And he views the history of the period as a "series of attempts to deal with the loss of these physical symbols of identity [king and court]."[9]

Morgan maintains that postexilic Israel developed a new "mindset." Jacob Neusner asserts that the people persevered because they were consumed with "an obsessive self-consciousness."[10] Walter Brueggemann contends that they engaged in an imaginative process of "world-building."[11] James Sanders writes that ancient Israel survived because it found a "dynamic source of identity."[12] Whether we call it "mindset," "obsessive self-consciousness," "world-building," or "source of identity," postexilic Israel redefined "nationhood" and found a way to remain a

---

[9]Donn F. Morgan, *Between Text and Community: The "Writings" in Canonical Interpretation* (Minneapolis: Fortress Press, 1990) 32.

[10]Jacob Neusner, *Self-Fulfilling Prophecy: Exile and Return in the History of Judaism* (Atlanta: Scholars Press, 1990) 9.

[11]Walter Brueggemann, *Israel's Praise: Doxology against Idolatry and Ideology* (Philadelphia: Fortress Press, 1988) 13.

[12]Sanders, "Adaptable for Life: The Nature and Function of Canon," in *From Sacred Story to Sacred Text*, 18.

separate and identifiable entity within the vast empires of which it found itself to be a part.

How? Why did Israel survive when the nations all around did not? Israel survived because the people interpreted and shaped their traditional and cultic material into a constitutive document of identity—the Hebrew scriptures. And they found in those texts, including the Psalter, a hermeneutical rationale for survival.

The Psalter is shaped traditionally into five books which narrate a history of ancient Israel. Books One and Two celebrate the reigns of David and Solomon; Book Three laments the dark days of oppression during the divided kingdoms and the Babylonian exile; and Books Four and Five look forward to and rejoice in Israel's restoration to the land and in the reign of YHWH as king. With the surety of the story of the Psalter (and the story in the rest of the Hebrew scriptures), the postexilic Isralite community could continue to exist as an identifiable entity in a world it no longer controlled.

Defining Terms

When we talk about the "shape and shaping" of the Psalter (or any book or collection of books in the scriptures), we are faced with two approaches to the text(s). When we speak of the "shape" of the Psalter, we think of Brevard Childs's method of "canon criticism," which seeks to understand the final, canonical shapes of the texts of the Hebrew Bible.[13] As Childs is quick to point out, the method does not ignore the results of historical-critical analysis, but its overarching concern is to understand the text as it is preserved for us.

The term "shaping" of the Psalter centers on James Sanders's method of "canonical criticism." This method seeks to uncover the process by which the texts of the Hebrew Bible reached their final, canonical form.[14] As with Childs's method, Sanders's does not ignore the results of

---

[13]Brevard S. Childs, "Reflections on the Modern Study of the Psalms," in *Magnalia Dei: The Mighty Acts of God*, ed. F. M. Cross et. al. (Garden City NY: Doubleday, 1976) 377-88; idem, *Introduction to the Old Testament as Scripture*; *Biblical Theology in Crisis* (Philadelphia: Westminster Press, 1970).

[14]See James A. Sanders, *Canon and Community: A Guide to Canonical Criticism*, GBS (Philadelphia: Fortress Press, 1984); and idem, *From Sacred Story to Sacred Text*.

historical-critical analysis, but seeks primarily to understand the process by which texts were preserved for us. The "shaping" of the final form of the Psalter, which was almost certainly accomplished in the postexilic period of ancient Israel's history, is the concern of this study.

Childs's "canon criticism" and Sanders's "canonical criticism" depart from the historical-critical methods in that they both focus on the texts as they stand within the canon of scripture, rather than on the texts' underlying forms, histories, or traditions. But Childs's basic concept of text is different from Sanders's. Childs understands text as the final form within the Hebrew or Christian Bible—the literary text. Sanders understands text as the result of a process of selection and appropriation by historical communities. Canonization is an active and dynamic process, and text shapes community as much as community shapes text.[15] The text is not static, but an active participant in the community of faith. Thus, the Hebrew scriptures reflect the hermeneutical underpinnings of the communities which "shaped the shaping" of the texts.

Approach

If we take seriously the advice of the King of Hearts about how to read a written work, then we must "begin at the beginning." The psalms located at the beginnings of each of the five books of the Psalter—Psalms 3, 42, 73, 90, and 107—should provide important clues about the book's "shaping," the process by which the postexilic community formed the Psalter, and about how we should read the work.

Psalm 3, which stands at the beginning of Book One's Psalms of David, is a typical lament of David, an "old, tried, and true" psalm which gives its readers a solid introduction to the subject matter of Book One. David's laments are the focus of Book One, and by means of Psalm 3, the reader/hearer understands how to approach the remainder of the psalms within it. Psalm 42, which opens Book Two, is a lament from the collection of the Psalms of the Sons of Qorah. David is still present in Book Two, but he is not as prominent as in Book One. Psalm 42 combines powerful imagery with admonitions to remember (vv. 5, 7) and to

---

[15]Sanders, *Canon and Community*, 21-45, and "Adaptable for Life: The Nature and Function of Canon," 11-39.

wait for YHWH (vv. 6, 12) as the psalmist dialogues with self, with נפשׁ, about whether to continue to trust in YHWH. Psalm 73, sometimes called the "Little Job" of the Psalter, is a fitting introduction to Book Three. It laments Israel's circumstances in exile. The old foundations of existence—David, the monarchy, and the land—are gone. Israel, like Job, must find new foundations upon which to base its relationship with YHWH.

Psalm 90 is the only psalm in the Psalter ascribed to Moses. The "shapers" of the Psalter placed this psalm at the beginning of Book Four in order to turn the reader's/hearer's attention away from David and the monarchy and back to the beginning, back to the "honeymoon" period of ancient Israel's relationship with YHWH—the Exodus—and back to the beginning of the Psalter. The key to Israel's survival in exile is precisely what it was in the Exodus—complete reliance upon YHWH. Psalm 107, which is placed at the beginning of Book Five, opens with praise to YHWH for gathering the redeemed from the East, the West, the North, and the South, and then goes on to describe the deeds of YHWH in very "kingly" language.

Each of these psalms functions in an important way in shaping the story of the Psalter. The circumstances of life in the postexilic community determined how the people read each psalm and/or group of psalms and the hermeneutical process by which the Psalter achieved its final shape.

If Book One of the Psalter celebrates the reigns of David and Solomon, then we may suggest that Psalm 3 introduces David, the ideal king of the golden age of Israel's history. Psalm 42, at the beginning of Book Two, reminds the reader/hearer that all was not well, even in the days of David and Solomon. But like David and Solomon, the reader can hope in YHWH in the midst of present despair. Book Three mourns the dark days of oppression and the Babylonian exile. At its beginning is Psalm 73, a lament that describes a situation in which all the old foundations of confidence are gone. The one good that remains is that YHWH is near.

Books Four and Five look forward to and rejoice in Israel's restoration to the land and in the reign of YHWH as king. Psalm 90 opens Book Four with expressions of great confidence in YHWH, and it never mentions King David. Psalm 107, at the beginning of Book Five, celebrates ancient Israel's return from exile and extols the benefits of YHWH as king. The story of the shaping of the Psalter is the story of the shaping of survival. The community shaped the text in order to give itself a rationale for continued existence, and the text shaped a community that survived the uncertainties of vassal existence. Thus, indeed, the community shaped the text and the text shaped the community.

The Canonical Method

Brevard S. Childs

Brevard Childs deserved a lion's share of the credit for twentieth-century scholarship's interest in canon. In a 1976 article titled "Reflections on the Modern Study of the Psalms," he observed that scholars had made no new advances in the fields of form-critical and cult-functional analysis of the Psalter during the previous two decades.[16] He maintained that the time had come to turn away from studying the "original setting" of the psalms and to emphasize instead their "canonical setting."[17] Childs accepts the importance of the foundational work of scholars like Gunkel and Mowinckel, but he maintains that their methodologies have disclosed just about as much information about the psalms as they are able, and that the law of diminishing returns has set in upon traditional biblical scholarship.

Childs developed a method he calls "canonical analysis," also known as "canon criticism,"[18] which he models in his 1979 *Introduction to the*

---

[16]Childs, "Reflections on the Modern Study of the Psalms," 378.

[17]Ibid., 378-79. He writes:

Much of the exegetical gain of determining the original setting of a psalm is jeopardized when the proposed *Sitz im Leben* rests on an extremely fragile and hypothetical base. Moreover, the function of a secondary setting often seems to be more significant for exegesis than a fixation with an alleged original *Sitz*. . . . [Therefore,] at least for an increasing number of scholars the problem of understanding the present shape of the Psalter emerges as a more pressing problem than the reconstructed original form of the text.

[18]Childs dislikes referring to his method as "canonical criticism" or "canon criticism" because he doesn't want his approach viewed as just the next criticism. He maintains that it is a totally new departure, *replacing* the entire historical-critical method. See Childs, *Introduction to the Old Testament as Scripture*, 82-83. John Barton prefers to call Childs's method "canon criticism," and I will adopt his nomenclature. See John Barton, *Reading the Old Testament* (Philadelphia: Westminster, 1984) 221.

Old Testament as Scripture. Canonical analysis, or canon criticism, focuses on the final form of texts; it seeks to use the Hebrew scriptures neither as a source of "other" information nor to reconstruct a history of ancient Israelite religious development.[19] Childs characterizes the method as "a descriptive one," since it seeks to understand the peculiar shapes and special functions of the texts that comprise the Hebrew scriptures.[20]

He points out that the final form of the Hebrew scriptures is what the ancient Israelites preserved, not the underlying layers of tradition of which it consists. Therefore, the best critical method for understanding its message is to study its final shape—that which "became normative for all successive generations of this community of faith."[21] He argues that scholarship cannot discover the history of the development of the canon because scribes and editors deliberately obscured the history of the "shaping" of the texts in a process Childs calls "actualization." Actualization is not just updating the past, but transmitting traditions in such a way as to prevent their "being moored in the past."[22]

In addition, the scribes and editors usually obscured their own identities. Childs asserts that who the editors and scribes were and how their particular histories influenced them, while perhaps interesting in the study of the Hebrew scriptures, simply cannot be known. And, therefore, the main focus of critical research should not lie in pursuing the editors' "motivations and biases."[23] Childs does not deny the need to investigate any historical influences on the canonical shapers to the extent that they can be determined. But, he writes, "Unfortunately we know so little about their work that many theories have been exceedingly speculative and largely unproductive up to now."[24]

This "fact" acts as one of the parameters for interpretation. The texts are to be a direct witness to God rather than a revelation of Israel's growing self-identity. It is not the *process* that is to function as the norm

---

[19]Childs, *Introduction to the Old Testament as Scripture,* 73.
[20]Ibid., 72.
[21]Ibid., 75.
[22]Ibid., 79.
[23]Brevard S. Childs, "Response to Reviews of *Introduction to the Old Testament as Scripture,*" JSOT 16 (1980): 54.
[24]Ibid.

for interpretation, but the product of the process.[25] The final form of the texts, not the transmission processes of the texts' editors, is the key to understanding the texts.

In the case of the Psalter, Childs maintains that the canonical form of the text looses the psalms from their cultic settings and makes them testify to the common troubles and joys of ordinary human life in which all persons participate.[26] Regardless of the intent of the editors and redactors of the Psalter, the end product has a universalized shape.

An example of Childs's approach is his analysis of the super-scriptions in the Psalter.[27] Seventy-three of the psalms in the Psalter are directly ascribed to David and thirteen psalms locate themselves, in their superscriptions, in particular historical settings in the life of David.[28] Childs writes that scholars in general ignore the superscriptions because they consider them late additions to the Psalter that offer little in the way of helping to establish genuine historical settings for the psalms. Childs agrees with this analysis; he states that the most important factor in the formation of the titles appears to be not precise references in the psalms to incidents in David's life, but "general parallels between the situations described in the psalms and some incidents in the life of David."[29]

He maintains that the psalm titles "unlock" David's inner life for readers and open to them David's "inner thoughts and reflections." "The titles established a secondary setting which became normative for the canonical tradition."[30] The canonical text takes psalms that once functioned within the cultic context and historicizes them by placing them within the history of David. The titles move the psalms out of their cultic setting and into the history of ancient Israel. In addition, the incidents from the life of David which appear at the beginnings of various psalms do not represent royal occasions or pictures of a very "kingly" David. The incidents portray David as someone who is chosen by YHWH, but who displays all the strengths and weaknesses of a human being.[31]

---

[25]Childs, *Introduction to the Old Testament as Scripture*, 75-76.

[26]Ibid., 521.

[27]Brevard S. Childs, "Psalm Titles and Midrashic Exegesis," JSS 16 (1971): 137-50; and *Introduction to the Old Testament as Scripture*, 520-22.

[28]See Psalms 3, 7, 18, 34, 51, 52, 54, 56, 57, 59, 60, 63, and 142.

[29]Ibid., 147.

[30]Ibid., 137.

[31]Childs, *Introduction to the Old Testament as Scripture*, 521:

James A. Sanders

James Sanders shares Brevard Childs's interest in studying the final form of the Hebrew scriptures. In 1977, Sanders voiced his own call for a reevaluation of the way scholars approach the biblical texts.

> The biblical story has become eclipsed by the work of the very professionals in seminaries and departments of religion who seem to know most about the Bible. In the rhetoric of today, the experts have lost perspective on the very object of their expertise. . . . [Biblical criticism] has reduced the Bible to grist for the historian's mill, the province of the professor's study.[32]

Although Sanders, like Childs, finds nothing inherently wrong with historical-critical approaches to the biblical texts, he too maintains that scholars have lost perspective on the texts because they seek to trace them back to their individual oral forms (*Urtexte*) and authors, rather than to study them in their canonical form. According to Sanders, historical criticism has "focused in good, modern Western fashion" on individual authors, has fragmentized the text, and has locked the text in the past.[33]

Sanders does differ from Childs, however, in his approach to the canonical form of the texts. Childs views the biblical texts as fixed entities that can be approached and studied only in their final, literary form. Scholars need not try to discover the historical settings of the texts because the editorial process Childs calls "actualization" has updated texts in such a way that their historical "moorings" are completely obscured and cannot be known.[34] He asserts that this is the reason attempts to describe the historical backgrounds of the biblical texts have been "exceedingly speculative and largely unproductive."[35]

The effect of this new context has wide hermeneutical implications. The psalms are transmitted as the sacred psalms of David, but they testify to all the common troubles and joys of ordinary human life in which all persons participate. These psalms do not need to be cultically actualized to serve later generations. They are made immediately accessible to the faithful.

[32]Sanders, "Biblical Criticism and the Bible as Canon," in *From Sacred Story to Sacred Text*, 78-79.

[33]Sanders, "Canonical Context and Canonical Criticism," 163.

[34]Childs, *Introduction to the Old Testament as Scripture*, 79.

[35]Childs, "Response to Reviews of *Introduction to the Old Testament as*

Sanders, on the other hand, acknowledges that biblical texts are grounded in historical settings, that those settings can be discovered, and that they are important for understanding the canonical shape of the texts. But he maintains that scholars have looked in the wrong places for those historical settings. The underpinnings of the biblical texts are located in communities of faith, not in individual scribal settings. This is the dimension or perspective that historical-critical scholarship has overlooked—that communities, not individuals, preserved and transmitted the biblical texts over the millennia. The way to understand the hermeneutical underpinnings of the texts is to understand those communities. Sanders describes his method of "canonical criticism" as follows:

> There has been a relationship between tradition, written and oral, and community, a constant, ongoing dialogue, a historical memory passed on from generation to generation, in which the special relationship between canon and community resided.[36]

Communities found value in the texts of which the Bible is composed or those texts would not have been preserved. The texts gave life, at crucial junctures in their transmissions, to the generations of communities that read them and sought answers in them to their existential needs.[37] And thus, through a process of selection and use, certain texts became part of the corporate tradition of the people—that is, they became normative and authoritative. When biblical scholarship focuses on individual authors and underlying texts, it shifts attention away from what the communities received, appropriated, and passed on, and it misses the important dimension of the shaping community.

Community is the foundation of canon. Discovering the hermeneutics of the communities that shaped the authoritative traditions into canon is the foundation of canonical criticism. And according to Sanders, those hermeneutics cannot be discovered without as much knowledge as possible of the ancient historical contexts.[38]

Sanders points out that Childs especially misses this dimension in one aspect of his analysis of the Hebrew Psalter. Childs may be correct in

Scripture," 54.

[36]Sanders, "Canonical Context and Canonical Criticism," 166.

[37]Sanders, "Biblical Criticism and the Bible as Canon," 82.

[38]Ibid., 83.

claiming that the community which shaped the Hebrew Psalter connected various psalms with specific events in the life of David in order to show David as a typical person with whom God was dealing in everyday events.[39] But the community's editors drew attention to very specific events in the life of David—situations with which they expected their readers to be familiar. Sanders writes:

> Does not most such editorial work indicate the intense interest of such redactors in date lines and historical contexts? They seem to be saying fairly clearly, if the reader wants to understand the full import for his or her (later) situation of what Scripture is saying, he or she had best consider the original historical context in which this passage scored its point.[40]

Sanders aptly demonstrates that Childs's concept of "actualization" is far too simplistic for the complex and multifarious texts of the Hebrew scriptures. The historical situations of the communities which preserved and transmitted the biblical texts *did* affect their task and we *can* discover their "footprints" in the canonical text.

Canonization takes place in community through a long process of selection and repetition of traditions. The process begins when an idea or story passes "the immense barrier from a first telling to a second."[41] As the idea or story is repeated in the community, it changes and updates, even if imperceptibly. Sanders maintains that when people repeat an idea or story, they may be able to do it verbatim, but the very fact that the later context of telling and hearing involves different participants, different questions, and different concerns gives the story a new, and sometimes different, meaning.

Ideas and stories can only cross the barrier from a first telling to a second—and thus become tradition—if they are able to meet new needs, to answer questions, in new situations. Otherwise they will not continue to be selected, repeated, and preserved by succeeding communities. That is their authority. And traditions become authoritative when they are able

---

[39]See Psalms 3, 7, 18, 34, 51, 52, 54, 56, 57, 59, 60, 63, and 142; Childs, "Psalm Titles and Midrashic Exegesis," 137-50; and idem, *Introduction to the Old Testament as Scripture*, 520-22.

[40]Sanders, "Canonical Context and Canonical Criticism," 170.

[41]Sanders, "Adaptable for Life: The Nature and Function of Canon," 16.

to provide answers to two basic existential questions: "Who are we?" and "What are we to do?"[42]

Ancient Israel and early Judaism repeatedly asked these questions of, and found answers in, their traditions. Jacob Neusner maintains that, in fact, ancient Israel had a "persistent passion for self-definition."[43] The people continually asked, "Who are we and what are the rules that define Israel as a social and political entity?" The communities' abilities to find answers in their traditions is the key to the survival of ancient Israel and early Judaism. The people achieved both stability—by finding answers to the question "Who are we?"—and adaptability—by finding answers to the question "What are we to do?"

Unless we understand the historical backgrounds to the questions and the answers, we cannot understand the hermeneutical underpinnings of the biblical texts. Sanders summarizes the point well:

> Why did Israel survive? That is the immense historical question that begs explanation. That which happened to some other victim nations [of Babylonian, Persian, Greek, or Roman expansion] did not happen to Israel. Israel changed rather radically, to be sure, from being a nation with its own government and a highly nationalistic cult, to a dispersed religious community called Judaism. But the point is that Israel survived whereas others did not.[44]

Ancient Israel and early Judaism survived because they found answers to the vexing problems of maintaining identity and direction in the tumultuous world of which they found themselves a part. The people collected, studied, appropriated, and edited their traditions into answers to the questions and problems that surrounded them.

---

[42]James A. Sanders, *Torah and Canon* (Philadelphia: Fortress Press, 1972) xv.

[43]Neusner, *Self-Fulfilling Prophecy*, 9.

[44]Sanders, "Adaptable for Life: The Nature and Function of Canon," 18.

Chapter 2

A History of Canon

Canonization takes place when communities decide a text or group of texts should be preserved and passed along unchanged. At some point in the transmission process, the ancient Israelite and early Jewish communities determined that certain forms of their authoritative texts were "decisive," and they chose to make no further updates to them. The texts had normative authority, so subsequent redaction either was thought unnecessary or did not find favor in the community.

But it is important to keep in mind that the actual term "canon"[1] is not used in connection with the biblical text until relatively late, and then first by Christian writers. In 367 CE the Alexandrian theologian Athanasius, in his thirty-ninth Easter letter, published a list of books that were to constitute the "canon" of the Christian Church. Thirty years later, in 397, the Third Council of Carthage acknowledged the same books as canonical.

At the turn of the Common Era, Judaism had no canon, no officially sanctioned list of "authoritative scriptures." However, the writers of the New Testament documents clearly indicate that some sort of authoritative body of Jewish literature did exist. John 13:18 and Galatians 3:8 refer to "the scripture" (ἡ γραφή). Paul speaks of "the Law" (ὁ νόμος) in 1 Corinthians 14:21. Matthew 7:12 calls this body of literature "the Law and the Prophets" (ὁ νόμος καὶ οἱ προφῆται). Luke 24:27 names it "Moses and all the Prophets" (Μωϋσέως καὶ πάντες οἱ προφῆται). And in a single instance in Luke 24:44, Jesus refers to "the law of Moses and the Prophets and Psalms" (ὁ νόμος Μωϋσέως καὶ οἱ προφῆται καὶ ψαλμοῖς).

---

[1]A "canon" is defined as a standard list of writings officially accepted by a church or religious body as genuine and normative.

The title "Psalms" in Luke 24:44 may mean simply what it says—the Psalter of Jewish worship. Or it may have been used to designate the whole of the כתובים (the Writings), at least that part of the whole which had been compiled by the time Luke wrote. Whatever Luke may have intended about the contents of "Psalms," it is clear that the author knew of a third section of scripture beyond "the Law and the Prophets."

If we acknowledge that the author of Luke knew of a three-part body of Jewish scripture, then was there a Jewish canon of scripture in the first century CE? John Barton, in *Oracles of God*, defines "scripture" and "canon" in terms of a distinction between a broad and narrow view of what constitutes normative literature. The word "scripture" signifies a broad view. "To speak of 'scripture'," he writes, "is to say that there is a group of books such that *at least* those books have an authoritative status."[2] The word "canon" narrows the focus. "To speak of 'canon' is to say that *at most* this particular group of books has authoritative status."[3] A. C. Sundberg suggests that we should understand "by 'scripture' religious writing that is in some sense authoritative, and by 'canon' a closed collection of scripture."[4] Just how "closed," then, was the Jewish collection of scriptures in the first century CE?

The Wisdom of Jesus ben Sirach, or Ecclesiasticus, was translated into Greek by the original author's grandson in the late second century BCE. In the prologue to the translation the translator declares that

> Many great teachings have been given to us through the law and the prophets and the others who followed them. . . . My grandfather Jesus devoted himself especially to the reading of the law—τοῦ νό- μου—and the prophets—τῶν προφητῶν—and the other books of our fathers—τῶν ἀλλώ πατρίων βιβλίων— . . . .

The passage suggests that the translator knew of three groups of documents in the Hebrew scriptures and implies that the original author also knew of such a breakdown, although the text gives no information about what specifically was included in the three sections.

---

[2] John Barton, *Oracles of God: Perceptions of Ancient Prophecy in Israel after the Exile* (London: Darton, Longman, and Todd, 1986) 56.

[3] Ibid.

[4] A. C. Sundberg, "The 'Old Testament': A Christian Canon," CBQ 30 (1968) 147.

A century and a half after the translation of the Wisdom of Jesus ben Sirach, Josephus the Jewish historian wrote *Against Apion*, an apologetic work directed to the Gentiles. In *Against Apion*, Josephus observes:

> For we [the Jews] have not an innumerable multitude of books among us, disagreeing from and contradicting one another, [as the Greeks have,] but only twenty-two books, which contain the records of all the past times; which are justly believed to be divine; and of them five belong to Moses, which contain his laws and the traditions of the origin of mankind till his death. . . . the prophets, who were after Moses, wrote down what was done in their times in thirteen books. The remaining four books contain hymns to God, and precepts for the conduct of human life.[5]

Thus Josephus fixes the number of books in the Jewish canon at twenty-two: five books of Moses, thirteen books of the prophets, and four books of hymns and maxims for life.

The Babylonian Talmud tractate *Bava Batra* gives a full list of the Jewish scriptures:

> Moses wrote his own book, and the section about Balaam and Job. Joshua wrote his own book, and eight verses in the Torah. . . . Our rabbis taught that the order of the prophets is Joshua, Judges, Samuel, Kings, Jeremiah, Ezekiel, Isaiah, the Twelve. . . . The order of the Hagiographa is Ruth, Psalms, Job, Proverbs, Ecclesiastes, Song of Songs, Lamentations, Daniel, Esther, Ezra, Chronicles. (*Bava Batra* 14b)

While the Babylonian Talmud dates from 600 CE, the formula "our rabbis taught" indicates that what follows was an oral tradition which originated sometime before 200 CE.[6] With some variations in the divisions of the canon and in the sequence of certain books (that is, Isaiah, Ruth, Song of Songs, and Esther), the list in *Bava Batra* agrees with the Masoretic Text.

---

[5]Flavius Josephus, *Against Apion*, in *The Works of Josephus*, trans. William Whiston (Peabody MA: Hendrickson Publishers, 1987) 1.38-40, 776.

[6]See E. Earle Ellis, "The Old Testament Canon in the Early Church," in *Mikra: Text, Translation, Reading and Interpretation of the Hebrew Bible in Ancient Judaism and Early Christianity*, ed. Martin Jan Mulder (Philadelphia: Fortress Press, 1988) 660.

The Qumran fragments of the Psalter provide additional evidence about the history of the "canon" of the Hebrew scriptures. More than thirty fragments of the Psalter have been found at Qumran, and, in all, they suggest that the content of the book was still relatively fluid well into the first century CE. Two important fragments come from cave 11 and cave 4.

In cave 11, the fragment known as 11QPs[a], probably copied during the time period 30–50 CE,[7] contains thirty-nine canonical psalms with other poetry intermixed. The order of the psalms on the scroll is as follows: 101–103, 109, 118, 104, 147, 105, 146, 148, 121–132, 119, 135–136, 145, 154, a noncanonical psalm, 139, 137–138, the Wisdom of ben Sirach 51:13-30, a noncanonical psalm, 93, 141, 133, 144, 155, 142–143, 149–150, a noncanonical psalm, 2 Samuel 23:7, a prose statement about David's compositions, 140, 134, and 151 A and B.[8] After examining other scroll fragments, scholars conclude that, despite a rather haphazard ordering of the psalms, all of the psalms from Psalm 118 to Psalm 150 of the Masoretic Text are represented at Qumran except Psalm 120.[9]

From cave 4, scroll 4QPs[a] contains portions of Psalms 6–69. Unlike the psalms on the scroll in cave 11, these psalms follow almost exactly the order of the Masoretic Text. From this information, we can conclude that the order of the psalms in at least Books One and Two (containing Psalms 1–72) was fixed earlier than in Books Three, Four, and Five.[10] So while most (or all) of the psalms of the canonical Psalter were already a part of the collection of psalms used by the early Jewish community at

---

[7]James A. Sanders, *The Dead Sea Psalms Scroll* (Ithaca NY: Cornell University Press, 1967) 6.

[8]William L. Holladay, *The Psalms Through Three Thousand Years: Prayerbook of a Cloud of Witnesses* (Minneapolis: Fortress Press, 1993) 101; and Joseph A. Fitzmyer, *The Dead Sea Scrolls: Major Publications and Tools for Study* (Missoula MT: Scholars Press, 1975) 37-38.

[9]Holladay, *The Psalms Through Three Thousand Years*, 101, points out that Psalm 120 may have been present in 11QPs[a], on the lower portion of a column that is now missing. Psalm 120 has seven verses, and at the bottom of column xiv, seven verses of Psalm 135 are missing.

[10]See Sanders, *The Dead Sea Psalms Scroll*, 13-14; Holladay, *The Psalms through Three Thousand Years*, 101; and Gerald H. Wilson, *The Editing of the Hebrew Psalter*, SBLDS 76 (Chico CA: Scholars Press, 1985) 121.

Qumran, the final shape of the Psalter was not "firm" until at least the first century CE. This conclusion fits well with other evidence regarding the development of the canon.[11]

Based on the evidence from Qumran, the Talmud, Josephus, Ecclesiasticus, and the New Testament, we can trace a development from "scripture"—*at least* the law and the prophets in the second century BCE—to "canon"—*at most* the books listed in *Bava Batra* in the second century CE. Jewish sources do not speak of a "closing" of the canon, but rather of a time after which no subsequent writings were placed on an equal level with the scriptural books. Josephus writes in *Against Apion*:

> It is true our history hath been written since Artaxerxes, very particularly, but hath not been esteemed of the like authority with the former by our forefathers, because there hath not been an exact succession of prophets since that time; and how firmly we have given credit to those books of our own nation is evident by what we do; for during so many ages as have already passed, no one has been so bold as either to add

---

[11]Frank-Lothar Hossfeld and Erich Zenger, *Die Psalmen I, Psalm 1–50*, NEchtB (Würzburg: Echter Verlag, 1993) 8-9, suggest that the final redaction of the Book of Psalms was completed sometime around 200 BCE. They acknowledge that a number of scrolls of psalms were found at Qumran with discernibly different orders of psalms, but view them as various "editions" which represent parts of different liturgical collections of psalms, not a "canonical" psalter for the Qumran community. They also give a number of arguments for a complete Hebrew Psalter by 200–190 BCE, including: (1) the number of psalms, 150, remains fixed in both the Greek and Hebrew versions of the Psalter, even though the psalm divisions are different in each; and (2) Psalms 1, 2, and 149 are linguistically tied at an early date as introductions and conclusions to the Psalter.

I maintain that the Psalter achieved its "substantial" form sometime in the late Persian/early Greek period (late 4th century). The "story line" was in place by that time, but the "introduction" and "conclusion" and the actual content of Books Four and Five remained fluid for several centuries. Holladay, in *The Psalms through Three Thousand Years*, 134-46, suggests that Books One through Three (Psalms 1-89) were stabilized in form and content much earlier—sometime before the time of the Dead Sea Scrolls—than Books Four and Five (Psalms 90-150). He bases much of his argument on Wilson's work. I believe Holladay's and Wilson's analyses are essentially correct. See also Gerald H. Wilson, "A First Century CE Date for the Closing of the Hebrew Psalter?" in *Haim M. I. Gevaryahu Memorial Volume*, English-French-German Section, ed. Joshua J. Adler (Jerusalem: World Jewish Bible Center, 1990) 136-43.

anything to them or take anything from them, or to make any change
in them.[12]

Ancient Israel and early Judaism developed a sense of canon during
the five hundred years leading up to and during the first one hundred
years of the Common Era. What was there about this time that caused the
communities to move away from receiving, appropriating, and passing on
their traditions towards shaping them into fixed forms? What motivated
the community to move from "forming the footprints" to "fixing the
footprints"?

---

[12]Josephus, *Against Apion*, 1.41-42, 776.

Chapter 3

A History
of the Shaping Community

In 597, the Babylonian army carried Jehoiachin, the king of Judah, and many of his subjects into exile.[1] A decade later, the army sacked Jerusalem and destroyed the temple; the Davidic kingdom was at an end. But within fifty years, the Babylonian Empire was badly deteriorated and beset by socioeconomic, religious, and political problems. King Nabonidus (555–539), a military commander who came from the Syrian city of Haran, was not popular. Almost immediately after he became king, he tried to make the moon god Sin, rather than Marduk, the unifying god of Babylonia. The priests of Marduk and the general population of Babylon were alienated by Nabonidus's religious policy and his cultic "malpractice." The "Verse Account of Nabonidus" expresses the Babylonian priests' outrage at King Nabonidus:

> [. . . law (and)] order are not promulgated by him,
> [. . . *he made perish the common people* through w]ant,
>   the nobles he killed in war,
> [. . . for] the trader he blocked the road.

> [He had made the image of a deity] which nobody
>   had (ever) seen in (this) country
> [He introduced it into the temple] he placed (it)
>   upon a pedestal:
> [. . .] he called it by the name of Nanna,
> [. . . it is adorned with a . . . of lapis] lazuli,
>   crowned with a tiara.[2]

---

[1]See 2 Kings 25.

[2]James B. Pritchard, ed., *Ancient Near Eastern Texts Relating to the Old Testament*, 3rd ed. (Princeton: Princeton University Press, 1969) 312-13.

When the powerful new ruler King Cyrus II of Anshan appeared on the horizon, many in Babylon welcomed him as liberator and restorer of the cult of Marduk.[3] Evidence of Cyrus's positive image is also preserved in the biblical text. In Isaiah 41:21, the author writes that Cyrus "shall trample on rulers as on mortar, as the potter treads clay." And in 45:1, Cyrus is called "the anointed" of YHWH, who will "subdue nations before him and strip kings of their robes."

In 539, Babylon fell to Cyrus and the whole of the Babylonian Empire came under the rule of the Persian king. In the following year, Cyrus issued an edict that has come to be known as the "Cyrus Cylinder," in which he declares:

> I am Cyrus, king of the world, great king, legitimate king, king of Babylon, king of Sumer and Akkad, king of the four rims (of the earth), son of Cambyses . . . , great king, king of Anshan, grandson of Cyrus, great king, king of Anshan, descendant of Teispes . . . , great king, king of Anshan, of a family (which) always (exercised) kingship; . . .
>
> . . . (As to the region) from . . . as far as Ashur and Susa, Agade, Eshnunna, the towns Zamban, Me-Turnu, Der as well as the region of the Gutians, I returned to (these) sacred cities on the other side of the Tigris, the sanctuaries of which have been ruins for a long time, the images which (used) to live therein and established for them permanent sanctuaries. I (also) gathered all their (former) inhabitants and returned (to them) their habitations. . . .[4]

The book of Ezra (1:2-4 and 6:3-5) includes two portions of the restoration policy of Cyrus.[5] Ezra 6:3-5 states:

---

[3]J. Maxwell Miller and John H. Hayes maintain that three groups of people supported Cyrus's campaign to gain control of Babylon: (1) the Marduk priesthood; (2) the Babylonian merchants who had seen their markets disrupted and trade routes disappear; and (3) thousands of foreigners now living in Babylon who must have felt that chances for return to their homelands were better under anyone other than the ruling establishment. See Miller and Hayes, *A History of Ancient Israel and Judah* (Philadelphia: Westminster Press, 1986) 439.

[4]Pritchard, *Ancient Near Eastern Texts Relating to the Old Testament*, 316.

[5]Miller and Hayes assert that there is no reason to doubt the historical value of the texts in Ezra, "although their wording may have been shaped by the biblical editors." See Miller and Hayes, *A History of Ancient Israel and Judah*, 444-45.

Concerning the house of God at Jerusalem, let the house be rebuilt, the place where sacrifices are offered and burnt offerings are brought . . . let the cost be paid from the royal treasury. Moreover, let the gold and silver vessels of the house of God, which Nebuchadnezzar took out of the temple in Jerusalem and brought to Babylon, be restored and brought back to the temple in Jerusalem, each to its place; you shall put them in the house of God.

And Ezra 1:3-4 declares:

Any of those among you who are of his people—may their God be with them!—are now permitted to go up to Jerusalem in Judah, and rebuild the house of YHWH, the God of Israel—he is the God who is in Jerusalem; and let all survivors, in whatever place they reside, be assisted by the people of their place with silver and gold, with goods and with animals, besides freewill offerings for the house of God in Jerusalem.

Sometime after 538 BCE, a group of Jewish exiles made their way from Babylon to Jerusalem to begin the process of rebuilding the temple and molding ancient Judaism. By 515, the temple in Jerusalem was standing once again and was functioning as a cult center. The author of the book of Ezra recalls:

And this temple was completed on the third day of the month Adar; it was the sixth year of the reign of King Darius. And the sons of Israel, the priests, the Levites, and the rest of the exiles, celebrated the dedication of this house of God with joy. (Ezra 6:15-16)

The Persian emperor allowed the Jews to rebuild their temple and resume their religious practice. But their cultic ordinances could not interfere with or contradict the laws of the Persian Empire, and they remained vassals of the Persians.[6] Persia divided its vast empire into administrative districts called satrapies. Judah was part of the satrapy of Abar Nahara—"Beyond the River"—which lay west and south of the Euphrates and included Syria, Phoenicia, Palestine, and Cyprus, but it appears to have

---

[6]Gösta W. Ahlström, *The History of Ancient Palestine* (Minneapolis: Fortress Press, 1993) 816. He writes, "The Persian king had acknowledged Judah and its people as a 'nation,' which would be able to carry on its national religion as before, albeit now under Persian rule and supervision."

been a distinct unit within the satrapy and was ruled by a separately appointed governor, a *pehâ*.

Zerubbabel was probably one of these governors. He came to Jerusalem during the reign of Cyrus's son Cambyses (530–522) and was resident there during most of the restoration work on the temple. This time period is portrayed in the prophetic books of Haggai and Zechariah as one in which the Jewish community in Judah was in the process of organizing itself.

After the death of Cambyses in 522, the Persian Empire experienced turmoil and rebellion in many of its provinces, and Cambyses's successor, Darius I, worked for several years to consolidate his power. Jerusalem may have tried to take advantage of the turmoil and restore the preexilic Israelite kingdom of David in the person of Zerubbabel. Haggai 2:23 records:

> "On that day, I will take you, O Zerubbabel my servant, son of Shealtiel," says YHWH, "and make you like a signet ring, for I have chosen you," says YHWH of hosts.

Zechariah reports of Zerubbabel:

> The hands of Zerubbabel have laid the foundation of this house; his hands shall also complete it. . . . For whoever has despised the day of small things shall rejoice, and shall see the plummet stone in the hand of Zerubbabel. (4:9-10)

The background and identity of Zerubbabel are not clear. The Chronicler gives him a Davidic ancestry in 1 Chronicles 3:17-24. Perhaps Zerubbabel was an heir of the Davidic dynasty.[7] Perhaps he was a non-Davidic Jewish leader whom the Chronicler gave a royal lineage "in order to emphasize what the Chronicler considered to be essential—the continuity of the leadership in preexilic and postexilic times."[8] Whatever Zerubbabel's background, he seems to have become the focus of a dream of restoration of the Davidic empire in late sixth-century Jerusalem.

---

[7]Ibid., 840. Ahlström accepts the Chronicler's genealogy and maintains that the policy of the Persian Empire was to appoint provincial governors from among former ruling families. He writes that Zerubbabel would have been a good choice "even if he had no experience. He was of royal blood, and that is what counted."

[8]See Miller and Hayes, *A History of Ancient Israel and Judah*, 456.

Interestingly, Zerubbabel abruptly disappeared from the scene in post-exilic Jerusalem sometime around 519.[9] Darius I passed through Palestine about the same time on his way to put down a rebellion in Egypt, and we may ask, "Did the Persians assassinate Zerubbabel? Did they remove him from office and take him into exile? Or did he die coincidentally at that time?" Perhaps Zerubbabel had come too close to reestablishing the Davidic monarchy in Jerusalem and thereby threatened Persia's hold on this geographically strategic piece of land. Regardless of what happened to Zerubbabel, however, Darius I allowed the Jews to complete the restoration of the temple. And according to Ezra 6:15, it was dedicated in an official ceremony in 515 BCE. It seems the Persians continued their policy of allowing subject peoples to practice their own religions so long as they did not interfere or conflict with the laws of the Empire.

Darius I continued the work of expanding the Persian Empire begun by his predecessors. At its peak it stretched from the Indus Valley in southeast Asia to the Danube River in the Balkans, and from the steppes of southern Russia to Libya in North Africa. And Judah apparently remained firmly under Persian control. Extant texts tell us nothing about the Persian-appointed governors of Judah between Zerubbabel, who disappeared about 519, and Nehemiah, who arrived in Jerusalem in 445.[10]

Nehemiah came to Jerusalem as governor of the province during the reign of Artaxerxes I (465–424). According to the biblical text, he organized the rebuilding of the city wall and carried out various religious and social reforms, which included reinstating the position of the Levites in the temple (Neh 13:10-13), enforcing observation of the Sabbath (Neh 13:15-22), and taking measures to prevent Jews from mixing with "outsiders" in marriage (Neh 13:23-28).[11]

---

[9]The last mention of Zerubbabel is in Zechariah 4, which may date to February 519.

[10]I am following the chronology of Miller and Hayes, *A History of Ancient Israel and Judah*, 452-53, and Ahlström, *The History of Ancient Palestine*, 862-88, who date Nehemiah to 445 and Ezra to 398. Miller and Hayes, 462, point out that archaeologists have discovered a number of seals, bullae, and stamped jar handles with the names of other governors of Yehud on them. The governors were probably Jewish, with names such as Elnathan, Yehoezer, and Ahzai, and thus came from the local populace. But we do not know whether they preceded or followed Nehemiah.

[11]Ahlström maintains that Nehemiah played a key role in placing the temple

Ezra appeared on the scene in Jerusalem some fifty years later, in 398, during the reign of Artaxerxes II (405–359). He is described in Ezra 7:6 as "a scribe skilled in the law of Moses" and in 7:12 as "the priest, the scribe of the law of the God of heaven." He travelled to Jerusalem as a special commissioner of the Persian court to evaluate conditions in Jerusalem in light of "the law of God." Why did Artaxerxes II send Ezra to Jerusalem? Since another revolt against the Empire was stirring in Egypt, perhaps the Persian king wanted to strengthen his control of Judah in order to keep Egypt in check. In many ways, Artaxerxes II got more than that for which he bargained.

Ezra presented a law code to the Jewish people in a public reading (Neh 8:1-12), commanded them to observe the Feast of Tabernacles according to the code's stipulations (Neh 8:13-18), and secured a covenant from the people to obey the law code (Neh 9:38). Exactly what constituted Ezra's law code can no longer be determined. If the letter from Artaxerxes to Ezra recorded in Ezra 7:11-26 is authentic, then the law code Ezra brought with him was familiar to at least a portion of the population of Judah. Artaxerxes commanded Ezra to

> appoint magistrates and judges who may judge all the people in the province Beyond the River who know the laws of your God; and you shall teach those who do not know them. (Ezra 7:25)

The narrative in Ezra and Nehemiah suggests Ezra completed the process begun by Nehemiah of separating the "true" Israel from the remainder of the population of Judah. Only those who could trace their ancestry to the Jews who had been in exile in Babylon—the גולה—were true members of the nation "Israel." Those who had stayed in Judah—עם הארץ—were excluded from Ezra's newly constituted community.[12]

The early fourth century BCE marks the beginning of the hermeneutical process by which the postexilic community shaped the final form of its scriptures. Through a process of use and selection, Ezra's law code, along with other traditional and cultic material, was shaped into the

---

and the city of Jerusalem at the center of Jewish life in Judah. His various actions suggest that the temple had not been very important before Nehemiah's time. People had not come to grips with a "national" temple without a Judahite king. See Ahlström, *The History of Ancient Palestine*, 867.

[12]See Ezra 9:1-4 and 10:7-9.

Torah. During the same time, the community continued the shaping of other portions of the Hebrew scriptures, including the Psalter, and these texts also became authoritative.[13]

Scribes

Although the focus of canonical criticism is the community that shapes the traditional materials into authoritative scriptures, the tasks of preserving, copying, and handing on the written texts fell to a select group of people, the community scribes. Who were the scribes? And what role did they play in their communities?

Scribes had been an important part of the central administration of ancient Israel. They appear early in the reign of David[14] and were no doubt assigned the same kinds of duties as other scribes in the ancient Near East. Their duties would have included such things as drawing up economic inventories and transactions, drafting treaties and diplomatic correspondence, authoring royal annals, sending letter and edicts to the provinces, and preserving and transmitting literary and religious traditions.

Scribes almost always worked within the "establishment" in the ancient Near East, which means they were located in one of two arenas: the cult center—the temple—or the administrative center—the court. Therefore, we can surmise that the scribes responsible for shaping the "authoritative" literatures of Judaism probably came from the גולה—the returned exiles—not from עם הארץ—the people of the land.[15] And they would have been located in either the Jerusalem temple or the provincial governor's house.

---

[13]James Sanders defines authoritative literature as "material that bears repeating in a later moment both because of the need of the later moment and because of the value or power of the material repeated." Sanders, "Adaptable for Life: The Nature and Function of Canon," in *From Sacred Story to Sacred Text* (Philadelphia: Fortress Press, 1987) 21.

[14]See, e.g., 2 Sam 20:25.

[15]Philip R. Davies, *In Search of "Ancient Israel"*, JSOTSup 178 (Sheffield: Sheffield Academic Press, 1992) 107. Davies reminds us, though, "That does not prevent them from criticizing their own regime. There are texts in the Bible that contain quite trenchant denunciation. But this is always expressed in the words of an earlier prophet, so that no direct criticism of the current authorities is explicit."

In the case of the shaping of the Psalter—the shaping of ancient Israel's cultic "songs"—the temple, rather than the governor's house, is the most likely location for the scribal and editorial work. Who were the scribes of the second Jerusalem temple? According to Ezekiel, Chronicles, and the Priestly account in the Book of Numbers, the temple personnel were all members of the tribe of Levi, but they were stratified into the Aaronid priests and the Levites. The Levites occupied a subordinate position to the Aaronid priests. Numbers 3:6 says:

> Bring the tribe of Levi near and set them before Aaron the priest, that they may serve him. And they shall perform the duties for him and for the whole congregation before the tent of meeting, to do the service of the tabernacle. . . . You shall thus give the Levites to Aaron and to his sons; they are wholly given to him from among the children of Israel.

It seems that originally all the members of the tribe of Levi were set aside for special service to YHWH, but those who could show descent directly from Aaron—and from Zadok, according to Ezekiel—occupied higher positions within the cult than other Levites.[16] Nehemiah reestablished the Levites in the Jerusalem temple during his term as provincial governor.[17] But the Levites performed the more "menial" chores while the Aaronid priests came to be the ruling elite of the temple.

The Levites would be the most likely group within the postexilic community to collect, preserve, and "shape" the normative and authoritative songs of Israel's cult into the Psalter. They perhaps would have been a little closer to the common people and would have understood and reflected the hermeneutical foundations which underpinned the postexilic community. Whatever the antecedents of the levitical personnel at the postexilic temple, they, beginning at some time in the fourth century BCE, played a key role in the shaping of the Psalter and other portions of the Hebrew scriptures.

What were the factors that motivated the levitical scribes to shape the traditional and cultic materials of ancient Israel into the authoritative texts of the Hebrew scriptures? Remember that Persian policy allowed subject people a degree of self-rule and autonomy so long as they did not conflict with the Persian laws. The postexilic community lived in circum-

---

[16]See Ezek 44:10-16 and Neh 7:63-65.
[17]See Neh 13:10-13.

stances very different from that of its religious ancestors. The people were vassals, first to the Persians, then the Greeks, and then the Romans.

The days of King David and the nation of YHWH which stretched "from Dan to Beersheba" were long past. Temple and cult, not king and court, had to be the central focus of their "nationhood" and their source of identity. How could the people structure themselves to avoid being absorbed completely into the Persian, and later the Greek and the Roman, Empires? They survived because they turned their traditional and cultic literature into what P. R. Davies calls "a massive exercise in self-definition,"[18] what Walter Brueggemann calls an imaginative process of "world building,"[19] and what James Sanders calls "a dynamic source of identity."[20] The Hebrew Psalter is one portion of that source of identity.

What was the hermeneutical underpinning of the story of the Psalter? The postexilic Israelite community was vassal to one immense empire after another—the Persians, the Greeks, and the Romans. The people could not continue as a separate, identifiable entity in the only form they had known—as a nation with an independent king and court. The days of the Davidic monarchy were gone forever. Therefore, the key to survival was to transcend traditional ideas about nationhood and recognize YHWH as king over the new "religious nation" of Israel.

The postexilic community shaped the traditional and cultic material of ancient Israel and early Judaism into a constitutive "charter of existence"—the Hebrew scriptures. Why did Israel survive and the nations around it did not? Israel survived because it found in its authoritative texts, including the Psalter, a hermeneutical rationale for survival.

---

[18]Davies, *In Search of "Ancient Israel,"* 116.

[19]Walter Brueggemann, *Israel's Praise: Doxology against Idolatry and Ideology* (Philadelphia: Fortress Press, 1988) 13.

[20]Sanders, "Adaptable for Life: The Nature and Function of Canon," 18.

Chapter 4

A History of the Psalter

We cannot know the precise historical events by which the Hebrew Psalter achieved its final form. In this regard, Brevard Childs is correct in his observation that attempts to describe the historical backgrounds of the biblical texts have been "exceedingly speculative and largely unproductive."[1]

When the ancient Israelites returned from exile in Babylon in 538 BCE, they brought with them their Torah, their national history, and other texts which were part of their cultural and religious tradition. Psalms (תהלים, *tehillim*) appear to have been an integral part of the preexilic cult and continued to be important in the postexilic cult. Second Chronicles 29:20-36 gives the reader a postexilic look back at temple worship in the days of Hezekiah. Verses 26-30 suggest that singers, musical instruments, and songs—"with the words of David and Asaph the seer" (v. 30)—were an important part of the cult ritual. According to one of the oldest passages in the Mishnah (Tamid 7:4), the Levites in the temple sang a psalm for each day of the week. Another passage in the Mishnah states that the fifteen Songs of Ascents (Psalms 120–134) correspond to the fifteen steps of the temple. And the Talmud mentions that psalms were part of the temple services for New Moon, Rosh Hashanah, and Sukkoth.[2] To what extent the Psalter was drawn on for lections in the worship of the Jewish community is not clear, but we can be sure that the psalms

---

[1]Brevard S. Childs, *Introduction to the Old Testament as Scripture* (Philadelphia: Fortress Press, 1979) 54.

[2]See Simon Cohen, "Liturgical Psalms," in *Universal Jewish Encyclopedia*, vol. 9, ed. Isaac Landman (New York: Universal Jewish Encyclopedia Co., 1943) 18-19. See also Sigmund Mowinckel, *The Psalms in Israel's Worship*, vol. 1, trans. D. R. Ap-Thomas (New York: Abingdon Press, 1962) 2-3.

played a leading role both in singing in corporate worship and in private prayers. H.-J. Kraus calls the Psalter "the hymnal and prayer book of the postexilic congregation."[3]

The exact process by which the Book of Psalms came into existence is lost to the pages of history. Determining the identity of the individual authors of ancient Israel's psalms is as difficult as pinpointing dates and settings for their compositions. Kraus "assumes," based on biblical texts such as 2 Chronicles 29:20-36, that the vast majority of psalms was the work of priests and temple singers.[4] Donn Morgan, in *Between Text and Community: The "Writings" in Canonical Interpretation*, writes that the literature is the product of "sages, scribes, singers, prayers, community builders, visionaries, and storytellers."[5] Morgan's broad categorization seems to be, for now, the best approach to the question of authorship of the psalms.

A large number of psalms apparently circulated within ancient Israel's cultic life. A prose insert in the Dead Sea Psalms Scroll 11QPs[a] states that David composed some 4,050 psalms and songs.[6] The Deuteronomistic historian writes in 1 Kings 4:32 that the songs of Solomon were 1,005. The Septuagint and the Qumran scrolls contain psalms that are not part of the Masoretic Text of the Psalter, as do other books of the Hebrew scriptures. And the pseudepigraphic Psalms of Solomon contains eighteen psalms that bear a close resemblance to biblical psalms.[7]

---

[3]H.-J. Kraus, *Psalms 1–59: A Commentary*, trans. H. C. Oswald (Minneapolis: Augsburg Publishing House, 1988) 20.

[4]Ibid., 66.

[5]Donn F. Morgan, *Between Text and Community: the "Writings" in Canonical Interpretation* (Minneapolis: Fortress Press, 1990) 5.

[6]James A. Sanders, *The Dead Sea Psalms Scroll* (Ithaca NY: Cornell University Press, 1967) 87.

[7]William L. Holladay, *The Psalms through Three Thousand Years: Prayerbook of a Cloud of Witnesses* (Minneapolis: Fortress Press, 1993) 97.

Scribes or temple functionaries grouped together some compositions into small collections of like pieces.[8] We can detect the following "collections" within the canonical Psalter.

Davidic Collections	Pss. 3–41; 51–72; 138–145
Korahite Collections	Pss. 42–49; 84–85; 87–88
Elohistic Collection	Pss. 42–83 ?
Asaphite Collection	Pss. 73–83
Kingship of God Psalms	Pss. 93–100
Psalms of Praise	Pss. 103–107
Songs of Ascents	Pss. 120–134
Hallelujah Psalms	Pss. 111–118; 146–150[9]

Editors joined these collections into larger units and ultimately arrived at the 150-psalm, five-book arrangement of the Masoretic Text.

The five divisions of the Psalter is an early tradition in Judaism. The Psalms scrolls from Qumran are divided into five books.[10] The *Midrash Tehillim*, which contains very early material, such as the sayings of Rabbis Hillel and Shammai (ca. first century BCE), states in the commentary to Psalm 1:

As Moses gave five books of laws to Israel, so David gave five Books of Psalms to Israel, the Book of psalms entitled *Blessed is the man* (Ps. 1:1), the Book entitled *For the leader: Maschil* (Ps. 42:1), the Book, *A Psalm of Asaph* (Ps. 73:1), the Book *A Prayer of Moses* (Ps. 90:1), and the Book, *Let the redeemed of the Lord say* (Ps. 107:2).[11]

Gerald Wilson found significant clues to the shape of the Psalter in the closing psalm of each of the five books.[12] He maintains that the

---

[8]Claus Westermann, *Praise and Lament in the Psalms*, trans. K. R. Crim and R. N. Soulen (Atlanta: John Knox Press, 1981) 250-51, observes that "behind the Psalter, at least in part, there were collections uniform in content." Westermann bases his statement on a study of the Book of Lamentations which "proves that there once was in Israel a collection of Psalms uniform in subject matter."

[9]W. H. Bellinger, Jr., *Psalms: Reading and Studying the Book of Praises* (Peabody MA: Hendrickson Publishers, 1990) 10.

[10]Sanders, *The Dead Sea Psalms Scroll*, 14.

[11]William G. Braude, *The Midrash on Psalms*, vol. 1 (New Haven CT: Yale University Press, 1959) 5. Frank-Lothar Hossfeld and Erich Zenger, *Die Psalmen I, Psalm 1–50* (Würzburg: Echter Verlag, 1993) 9-11, discuss the origin and function of the five-book division of the Psalter.

[12]See Gerald H. Wilson, *The Editing of the Hebrew Psalter*, SBLDS 76

Hebrew Psalter is a story of the rise of ancient Israel under the leadership of Kings David and Solomon (Books One and Two); of the demise of ancient Israel, the destruction of Jerusalem at the hands of the Babylonians, and the Exile (Book Three); and of the return to the land and the time when YHWH would restore the fortunes of ancient Israel (Books Four and Five). Wilson is essentially correct, and his research has done much to initiate the move by biblical scholars to examine the process by which the Psalter achieved its final form. Other clues to the shaping of the Psalter also exist—clues that can be discovered by understanding the historical backgrounds and hermeneutical underpinnings of the postexilic community.

Books One, Two, and Three appear to have a different editorial history than Books Four and Five. There are a number of differences between Books One through Three and Books Four and Five. First, of the eighty-nine psalms in Books One, Two, and Three, all but six refer to an "author" in their superscriptions. Fifty-six of them name David as that "author," and an additional twenty-four are ascribed to members of David's and Solomon's royal courts. In contrast, only nineteen of the sixty-one psalms in Books Four and Five specify an "author," and only fifteen name David as the "author."

Second, Books One through Three are dominated by "lament" psalms, while Books Four and Five contain a greater number of "hymn" psalms. In Books One through Three, fifty-two of the psalms are laments and twenty-four are hymns. Books Four and Five contain fifteen psalms of lament and thirty-seven hymns.[13]

Third, the Dead Sea Scrolls indicate that the order of the psalms in the first three books was relatively fixed by the time of the composition of the Dead Sea documents. Scroll 4QPs[a] contains portions of Psalms 6 through 69, and the order of the psalms is, for the most part, the canonical order. The order of the psalms in Books Four and Five, however, appears to have remained fluid after the order of Books One, Two, and Three was fixed. Scroll 11QPs[a] contains all or part of thirty-nine canoni-

---

(Chico CA: Scholars Press, 1985).

[13]Bellinger, *Psalms: Reading and Studying the Book of Praises*, 45, 75, 81. The remaining twenty-two psalms in the Psalter are classified as royal and wisdom psalms. See ibid., 106 and 124.

cal psalms, beginning with Psalm 101 and ending with 150. But the order of the psalms in 11QPs[a] is very different from the canonical Psalter.[14]

In the chapters that follow, we will see how these clues provide valuable information about the shaping of the Hebrew Psalter. Why do we have these 150 psalms and why are they in this particular order? While we cannot know the precise historical processes behind the formation of the Psalter, we can study its hermeneutical logic. Therefore, despite the admonitions of Rabbi Eleazar and Joshua ben Levi, let us proceed in our study of the shaping of "David's Psalms."[15]

---

[14]For an analysis of scrolls 4QPs[a] and 11QPs[a], see William L. Holladay, *The Psalms through Three Thousand Years*, 99-102.

[15]William G. Braude, *The Midrash on Psalms*, vol. 1 (New Haven CT: Yale University Press, 1959) 49-50.

Chapter 5
Book One

Introduction

"Begin at the beginning," the king said, gravely.[1]

This chapter will examine the beginning Psalms of Book One of the Psalter. While Psalm 3 begins Book One's collection of Laments of David, it is preceded by two psalms that are generally accepted as "introductions" to the work. Both are untitled—rare in Books One, Two, and Three—and they both precede Book One's collection of "Psalms of David."[2] Gerald Wilson, in *The Editing of the Hebrew Psalter*, suggests that the shapers of the Psalter freely used individual untitled psalms at various junctures in the Psalter to provide introductions and transitions, and Psalms 1 and 2 seem to be used in precisely this way.[3]

Many maintain that Psalms 1 and 2 were incorporated into the Psalter as a single psalm of introduction and then separated into two psalms at a later time. Others have argued that they were always two psalms, and each was added separately to the Psalter.[4] What difference does either

---

[1]Lewis Carroll, *Alice in Wonderland*, 2nd ed. (New York: Norton, 1992) 94.

[2]See Psalms 3–41, all but two of which contain לדוד in their superscriptions. In the first three books of the Psalter, all but eight (Psalms 1, 2, 10, 33, 43, 66, 67, and 71) have superscriptions.

[3]Gerald H. Wilson, *The Editing of the Hebrew Psalter*, SBLDS 76 (Chico CA: Scholars Press, 1985) 173-81 and 204; and idem, "The Use of 'Untitled' Psalms in the Hebrew Psalter," ZAW 97 (1985): 404-13.

[4]For a full discussion, see John T. Willis, "Psalm 1—An Entity," ZAW 91 (1979): 381-401; Wilson, *The Editing of the Hebrew Psalter*, 204-209; and J. Clinton McCann, Jr., *A Theological Introduction to the Book of Psalms: The Psalms as Torah* (Nashville: Abingdon Press, 1993) 25-27 and 41-45.

option make in our analysis of the shaping of the Psalter? Every clue, every footprint left by the shaping community is crucial for understanding the final shape of the work.

An important piece of evidence regarding the question of the possible unity of Psalms 1 and 2 comes from the New Testament Book of Acts. In Acts 13:33 a number of manuscripts read:

> . . . as also it is written in the first psalm,
> "Thou art my son,
>   today I have begotten thee." (=Psalm 2:7)[5]

While the greatest number of manuscripts of the Book of Acts read "in the second psalm" at 13:33,[6] the variant readings require some explanation. We may posit that (1) the author of Acts and/or the scribes who copied the manuscripts knew of a form of the Psalter in which Psalms 1 and 2 were a single entity; (2) they knew of a form in which Psalms 1 and 2 were separate, but Psalm 1 was unnumbered; or (3) they knew of a form of the Psalter in which Psalm 1 was not yet included and Psalm 2 stood in the first position.

When we consider the possibility that Psalms 1 and 2 were originally a single psalm, the similarities between them are striking. In addition to their both being untitled "introductory" psalms, Psalm 1 begins with אשרי (v. 1) and Psalm 2 ends with אשרי (v. 12). Psalm 1 begins with a description of the דרך of the wicked and sinners, while Psalm 2 closes with a warning that the enemies of YHWH and of YHWH's anointed will perish in the דרך. And both contain the Hebrew verbal roots הגה (1:2, 2:1), אבד (1:6, 2:12), and ישב (1:1, 2:4).

Psalm 1 contrasts individual sin and disobedience (רשעים) with individual obedience (צדיקים), and Psalm 2 contrasts the corporate sin and disobedience of the nations with corporate obedience. But Psalm 1 is classified as a "wisdom" psalm, while Psalm 2 is a "royal" psalm.[7] The two psalms stand well individually and were most likely separate

---

[5]E.g., Codex Bezae Cantabrigiensis (d; fifth century) and Codex Gigas (gig; thirteenth century), certain Latin manuscripts according to Bede (eighth century), and the marginal reading in Codex Philadelphiensis (Ph^ms; twelfth century). See Willis, "Psalm 1—An Entity," 385.

[6]Codex Sinaiticus (א; fourth century), Codex Alexandrinus (A; fifth century), Codex Vaticanus (B; fourth century), etc. See Willis, "Psalm 1—An Entity," 385.

[7]See below, nn. 18 and 24.

compositions. The strong connections between them certainly may explain why they were selected together to introduce the Psalter, but not that they should be understood and interpreted as a single psalm.

When we examine the second possibility, that Psalm 2 was added to the Psalter before Psalm 1, we find differing opinions. H.-J. Kraus and Frank-Lother Hossfeld and Erich Zenger, for example, maintain that Psalm 1 was added as a preamble, an introduction, to the Psalter after Psalm 2, which was already in place.[8] But the fact is we have no existing manuscripts that contain Psalm 2 without Psalm 1.

The third possibility is that at one stage in the history of the Psalter, Psalm 1 was regarded as the "introductory psalm" and Psalm 2 as Psalm 1.[9] Benjamin Kennicott's eighteenth-century notes to Psalm Codices 157 and 168 read:

> Psalm 1 lacks a number, as if it is a preface; to the second is added a slightly larger א, as an indication of the first psalm: in the same manner also the third ב, fourth ג, etc.

> Psalm 1 is considered a *quasi* preface: because numeration by letters in the margin begins with א at the psalm [which] in our [Psalter] is the second, ב at the third, etc.[10]

The Babylonian Talmud tractate *Berakoth* indicates that the numbering of the Psalter began at Psalm 2. Also in *Berakoth*, the rabbis maintain that Psalm 19 was actually the eighteenth psalm of the Psalter:

> Seeing that this verse, *Let the words of my mouth be acceptable* [Ps. 19:15, EVV 19:14], is suitable for recital either at the end or the beginning [of the *t'fillah*], why did the Rabbis institute it at the end of the eighteen benedictions? . . . those eighteen psalms are really nine-

---

[8]H.-J. Kraus, *Psalms 1–59: A Commentary*, trans. H. C. Oswald (Minneapolis: Augsburg Pub. House, 1988) 15; and Frank-Lothar Hossfeld and Erich Zenger, *Die Psalmen I, Psalm 1–50*, NEchtB (Würzburg: Echter Verlag, 1993) 45.

[9]Willis, "Psalm 1—An Entity," 385-91. Willis cites extensive evidence from early Church writers which indicates that while the writers "were aware of Hebrew manuscripts which treated Psalms 1 and 2 as a single psalm, they also knew of Hebrew manuscripts that divided them into separate psalms, and they themselves followed the latter practice almost unanimously."

[10]See Wilson, *The Editing of the Hebrew Psalter*, 204. Wilson translates from *Vetus Testamentum Hebraicum cum Variis Lectionibus*, Tomus Primus, ed. Benjamin Kennicott (Oxford: Clarendon, 1776).

teen—*Happy is the man* [Ps 1] and *Why are the nations in an uproar* [Ps 2] form one chapter.[11]

The major evidence regarding the time from which Psalms 1 and 2 were part of the Psalter comes from the Qumran documents and from the Midrash Tehillim. Psalm 1 is not preserved in any of the extant scrolls of the Psalter from the Dead Sea. Portions of Psalm 2 appear in 11QPs^c (2:2-8) and 3QPs (2:6-7).[12] Neither of the two longest psalm scrolls contain Psalm 1 or Psalm 2. Scroll 11QPs^a begins with Psalm 101 and contains psalms from the latter part of the Psalter. Scroll 4QPs^a contains only Psalm 5:9 through Psalm 69, although the edges of the scroll are sufficiently damaged to allow that some text *did* precede Psalm 5:9.

Scroll 4QFlor, or 4Q174, an anthology of biblical "proof texts" for the coming of two messiahs, a Davidic or kingly messiah and an Aaronic or priestly messiah, provides some additional evidence about Psalms 1 and 2.[13] The text, which probably dates to the first century BCE, is a commentary on 2 Samuel 7:10; Exodus 15:17-18; 2 Samuel 7:11-14; Amos 9:11; Psalm 1:1; Isaiah 8:11; Ezekiel 44:10; Psalm 2:1; and Daniel 12:10, in that order.[14] So while no conclusive evidence exists that Psalm 1 was a part of the Psalter of the Dead Sea community and only fragmentary evidence indicates that Psalm 2 was included, 4QFlor indicates that both psalms were known by the community at the time of the writing of the Florilegium in the first century BCE.

The Midrash Tehillim, compiled beginning in the second century CE, contains much material that dates to well before the common era.[15] It has full commentaries on both Psalms 1 and 2, and the commentary on

---

[11]*The Babylonian Talmud: Berakoth*, ed. Rabbi Dr. I. Epstein, trans. Maurice Simon (London: Soncino Press, 1958) 50-51.

[12]Peter W. Flint, *The Psalters in the Scrolls and the Book of Psalms*, STDJ (Leiden: E. J. Brill, 1996) appendix 4.

[13]William L. Holladay, *The Psalms through Three Thousand Years: Prayerbook of a Cloud of Witnesses* (Minneapolis: Fortress Press, 1993) 102.

[14]Ibid., 102-103. For a complete analysis, see Willis, "Psalm 1—An Entity," 381-84, and George J. Brooke, *Exegesis at Qumran: 4QFlorilegium in Its Jewish Context*, JSOTSup 29 (Sheffield: JSOT Press, 1985).

[15]William G. Braude, *The Midrash on Psalms*, vol. 1 (New Haven CT: Yale University Press, 1959) xi. The sayings of Rabbis Hillel and Shammai, e.g., come from the first century BCE.

Psalm 1 includes the breakdown of the books of the Psalter, indicating its position as the beginning psalm of the Psalter:

> As Moses gave five books of laws to Israel, so David gave five Books of Psalms to Israel, the Book of Psalms entitled *Blessed is the man* (Ps. 1:1), the Book entitled *For the leader: Maschil* (Ps. 41:1), the Book, *A Psalm of Asaph* (Ps. 73:1), the Book, *A Prayer of Moses* (Ps. 90:1), and the Book, *Let the redeemed of the Lord say* (Ps. 107:2). Finally, as Moses blessed Israel with the words *Blessed art thou, O Israel* (Deut. 33:29), so David blessed Israel with the words *Blessed is the man.*[16]

The evidence from the Dead Sea sources indicates that Psalms 1 and 2 were at least known in the community, although we cannot determine whether they were a part of the Psalter. The Midrash Tehillim confirms that Psalms 1 and 2 were firmly fixed as the beginning psalms of the Hebrew Psalter from a fairly early time, certainly before the second century CE. And while Psalm 1 is unnumbered in some Hebrew Bible manuscripts, we have no manuscripts that do not contain Psalm 1 and no manuscripts in which Psalms 1 and 2 are combined, with no break between the two.

Therefore, we may conclude that Psalms 1 and 2 were added to the Psalter at about the same time during its shaping process, and both were initially considered as introductions to the text. Because of Psalm 2's subject matter, kingship, some communities linked it with Book One's collection of Psalms of David (Psalms 3–41) and separated it from its introductory position. In those communities, Psalm 1 remained an unnumbered introduction or prologue, and Psalm 2 became Psalm 1, prefacing Book One's laments of David. In other communities, both psalms remained as introduction and both were numbered. We turn now to these two psalms of introduction.

Psalm 1

Psalm 1 begins with אַשְׁרֵי הָאִישׁ ("Blessed/Happy the one"), a wisdom formula that calls readers/hearers to listen to the words that follow in order to find happiness or blessing.[17] Psalm 1 is usually classified as a

---

[16]Ibid., 5.

[17]Henri Cazelles suggests that אשרי occurs most often in late Hebrew texts, and he connects it with the liturgy of the Second Temple. Cazelles, אַשְׁרֵי *'ashrê*, in *Theological Dictionary of the Old Testament*, vol. 1 (Grand Rapids MI:

wisdom psalm, along with Psalms 32, 37, 49, 73, 78, 112, 119, 127, 128, and 133.[18] The psalm gives the source of happiness or blessing as the תורת יהוה (the Torah of YHWH). The one who "meditates" (הגה) upon the instruction, the תורת יהוה will yield fruit and prosper (v. 3).

תורה in Psalm 1 is not "the Law"—a set of rules which must be obeyed—with which many readers/hearers associate the word. It was a positive concept to the author of this psalm and to the community which placed Psalm 1 at the beginning of the Psalter. Torah, in its literary sense, is the whole of the five books of the Pentateuch—the history of ancient Israel as well as the laws given to the people. James L. Mays writes that "*torah* in Psalm 1 means instruction in the broadest sense, tradition that is authoritative for the people of God."[19] Torah is the central theme of Psalm 1 and an important introductory concept of the Psalter. But the Torah is the community's traditional memory of YHWH's complete involvement in the life of the people of ancient Israel. It is story plus instruction.

Meditating upon YHWH's instruction separates the צדיקים (the righteous ones) from the רשעים (the wicked ones). We encounter the רשעים in other psalms as the oppressors against which the psalmists lament.[20] Psalm 1 suggests that the way to overcome the רשעים is to delight in and

---

Eerdmans, 1974) 446.

[18]See W. H. Bellinger, Jr., *Psalms: Reading and Studying the Book of Praises* (Peabody MA: Hendrickson Publishers, 1990) 124; McCann, *A Theological Introduction to the Book of Psalms*, 25-40; Peter C. Craigie, *Psalms 1–50*, WBC 19 (Waco TX: Word Books, 1983) 57; and Kraus, *Psalms 1–59: A Commentary*, 112-15. Brevard S. Childs, *Introduction to the Old Testament as Scripture* (Philadelphia: Fortress Press, 1979) 513, classifies Psalm 1 as a "Torah Psalm," as does James Luther Mays in "The Place of the Torah-Psalms in the Psalter," JBL 106 (1987): 3-12. Hossfeld and Zenger, *Die Psalmen I, Psalm 1–50*, 45, also classify Psalm 1 as a "wisdom" psalm, and they point out that the psalm, whose first word begins with א (אשרי) and last word begins with ח (תאבד) is an "alphabetic acrostic" which "als 'Lebenslehre' geprägt ist und eine solche 'von A bis Z' bieten will."

[19]James L. Mays, *Psalms*, Interpretation: A Bible Commentary for Teaching and Preaching (Louisville: John Knox Press, 1994) 15.

[20]Patrick Miller, "The Beginning of the Psalter," in *The Shape and Shaping of the Psalter*, ed. J. Clinton McCann, Jr., JSOTSup 159 (Sheffield UK: JSOT Press, 1993) 88, claims that a major function of Psalm 2 read after Psalm 1 is the setting of the category of the wicked "under the rubric 'enemies'."

meditate on the תורת יהוה. The רשעים will be driven away like chaff (v. 4) and the צדיקים will be firmly planted and bear fruit and prosper (v. 3). Psalm 1 does not in any manner offer two options for paths of life for the reader/hearer. It clearly emphasizes that the only path is דרך צדיקים (the way of the righteous ones).[21]

The community which shaped the Psalter indicates by the positioning of Psalm 1 that the תורת יהוה upon which the people are to meditate is located in the story of the Psalter.[22] Psalm 1 calls its readers/hearers to listen to the instruction of YHWH found in the psalms of the Psalter. Its introductory position alters the function of the Psalter for postexilic ancient Israel. The psalms that had once been used as cultic songs *to* YHWH are now to be listened to as instruction *from* YHWH.[23] What is the content of the instruction of YHWH on which the צדיקים are to meditate and in which they are to find delight? Psalm 2 states that the first step is for the people to rely completely on YHWH to deliver them from their oppressors.

Psalm 2

Psalm 2 is categorized as a "royal" psalm, along with Psalms 18, 20, 21, 45, 72, 89, 101, 110, 132, and 144.[24] Form critics categorize the royal psalms not by their literary types, such as "lament" or "hymn," but by

---

[21]Hossfeld and Zenger, *Die Psalmen I, Psalm 1–50*, 45: "Sie werden freilich nicht als gleichwertige Alternativen dargestellt, wie besonders der Schlußsatz unterstreicht."

[22]Walter Brueggemann maintains, in fact, that the community's placement of Psalm 1 at the beginning of the Psalter "insists" upon a particular reading of the Psalter: "The Psalter begins in a confident summons to obedience which provides assurance about the consequence of obedience. Life revolves around torah and the obedience to which the torah summons Israel. . . . this Psalm (Psalm 1) intends that all the psalms should be read through the prism of torah obedience." See Walter Brueggemann, "Bounded by Obedience and Praise: The Psalms as Canon," JSOT 50 (1991): 64.

[23]Childs, *Introduction to the Old Testament as Scripture*, 513, writes, "The prayers of Israel directed to God have themselves become identified with God's word to his people." Gerald Wilson maintains that the Psalter in its final form is no longer simply a collection of cultic hymns, but that it is a book "to be read rather than performed, meditated over rather than recited from." See Wilson, *The Editing of the Hebrew Psalter*, 207.

[24]I am following the categorization of Bellinger in his *Psalms: Reading and Studying the Book of Praises*, 106-107.

their subject matter—the person of the king. The community that shaped the Psalter appropriated these royal psalms and placed them at various places in the Psalter, so that the psalms are "thoroughly scattered" throughout the text.[25]

We may marvel that the community that shaped the Psalter would preserve and include any royal psalms—psalms from the time of the Israelite monarchy—at all. The postexilic Israelites were living in Palestine, the land YHWH promised to Abraham and David, but they were under foreign domination and had no king of their own. Kingship had failed; the political state of "Israel" was no more. Would it not have been better to leave behind the failed aspect of ancient Israel's past and simply omit the royal psalms from the final collection? Certainly not all the psalms that circulated in preexilic and postexilic Israel were included in the Psalter.[26] But the shaping community *did* include these royal psalms, and they included them at a number of significant junctures in the Psalter. The "royal psalms," including Psalm 2, are part of the "footprints" of the shaping community. They provide the reader/hearer with more clues to the Psalter's hermeneutical underpinnings and the rationale for the shape of the text of the Psalter.

The Israelites of the postexilic period found themselves in circumstances very different from that of their ancestors. They were living as vassals of foreign nations, dependent for their future upon the policies of distant kings. Gone forever were the days of King David and the nation of YHWH which stretched "from Dan to Beersheba." For the ancient Israelites, the end of their royal dynasty meant the end of their political "state."[27] The people may well have asked questions like, "Are we still the people of YHWH?" "What is our status?" "How are we to survive without a king like David to lead us?" Psalm 2 provided the people with answers to these vexing questions.

Psalm 2 divides into four sections. Verses 1-3 describe conspiracy and plotting by nations, peoples, kings, and rulers against YHWH and YHWH's anointed. Psalm 2's use of the verb הגה immediately reminds the reader/hearer of Psalm 1. In verse 1 of Psalm 2 the psalmist writes that "peoples are meditating (or plotting) (יהגו) empty things." The same verb

---

[25]Childs, *Introduction to the Old Testament as Scripture*, 515-16.
[26]See chap. 4.
[27]See chap. 6.

is used in verse 2 of Psalm 1 to describe the manner in which a person should approach the instruction of YHWH: "and on his instruction he will meditate (יהגה) day and night."[28] The shaping community clearly differentiates the צדיקים (the righteous ones) of Psalm 1 with the nations, peoples, kings, and rulers of Psalm 2. Both are "meditating," but for very different purposes.

In verses 4 through 6, the scene changes to the heavenly realm where YHWH sits looking down upon the scene below. The psalmist uses powerful anthropomorphic imagery to describe YHWH's attitude toward those who are conspiring and plotting. YHWH laughs (שׂחק), scoffs (לעג), speaks in anger (דבר באף), and terrifies in fury (בהל בחרון). The nations, the peoples, the kings, and the rulers have no power over the situation.[29] Despite the empty meditating by the nations, YHWH will install (נסך) a king of divine choosing upon Zion.

In verses seven through nine the king recites the decree (חק) of YHWH, words which possibly were spoken at an actual enthronement ceremony in Jerusalem.[30] The חק יהוה was a document given to the king by YHWH during the king's coronation ceremony in Jerusalem. It renewed God's covenant commitment to the dynasty of David and established the nature and authority of the newly crowned king.[31] The content of the decree the psalmist relates is:

You are my son. Today I have begotten you. Ask of Me, and I will surely give the nations as your inheritance, and the end of the earth as your possession. (vv. 7, 8)

---

[28]McCann maintains that הגה in Psalms 1 and 2 "effectively contrasts" meditation on God's instruction with thinking that is empty or purposeless. See McCann, *A Theological Introduction to the Book of Psalms*, 41.

[29]Kraus sums it up well: "Behind the king of Jerusalem stands not any mythical power, but the Lord . . . who "mocks" the mad display of power on the part of the rebels. The vision of a laughing, mocking, heavenly Lord is a message of unheard-of prophetic force." See Kraus, *Psalms 1–59: A Commentary*, 128-29.

[30]Hossfeld and Zenger, *Die Psalmen I, Psalm 1–50*, 49, maintain that the order of the sections of Psalm 2 correspond to the ritual of an enthronement ceremony. See also James L. Mays, *The Lord Reigns: A Theological Handbook to the Psalms* (Louisville: Westminster/John Knox Press, 1994) 111-13.

[31]See 2 Kings 11:12 and Craigie, *Psalms 1–50*, 67. For a description of an enthronement ceremony, see Sigmund Mowinckel, *The Psalms in Israel's Worship*, vol. 1, trans. D. R. Ap-Thomas (New York: Abingdon Press, 1962) 61-76.

The words of YHWH's decree recited in Psalm 2 would bring to the mind of the postexilic community the covenant YHWH made with King David. The Deuteronomistic historian records in 2 Samuel 7:11-14 that YHWH spoke to David:

> YHWH will make a house for you. When your days are complete and you lie down with your fathers, I will raise up your descendant after you, who will come forth from you, and I will establish his kingdom forever. He shall build a house for my name, and I will establish the throne of his kingdom forever. I will be a father to him and he will be a son to me.[32]

YHWH promised that the throne of David would never be empty.

One prerogative of the royal offspring was the right to make requests of the god. Again, the postexilic community recalled David, who over and over in the laments of the Psalter and in the Deuteronomistic History sought YHWH's assistance and guidance through the difficulties of life. The psalms of petition individually and the Psalter as a whole may be seen as a reflection of David, the chosen, yet very imperfect, king of Israel. Terrence Collins, in a 1978 article in *The Journal for the Study of the Old Testament*, maintains that the Psalter is "a drama in miniature, which can only be fully appreciated when viewed as part of the large-scale drama of the worldview of Psalms and its understanding of human existence."[33] While Collins draws a much different conclusion about the "structure" of the Psalter than I do about its "shaping," his characterization is insightful.

The "drama in miniature" described in the Psalter is that of a community of people struggling to survive without the traditional underpinnings of existence. The solution at this time is:

> Serve YHWH with fear; with trembling kiss his feet.
> Lest he become angry and you perish in the way. (vv. 11, 12)

---

[32]The idea of the king being the offspring of the god—whether by blood or by adoption—is common throughout the ancient Near East. For a full discussion, see James W. Watts, "Psalm 2 In the Context of Biblical Theology," HBT 12 (1990): 75-78.

[33]Terrence Collins, "Decoding the Psalms: A Structural Approach to the Psalter," JSOT 37 (1987): 52.

For many scholars, the interpretation of verses 11 and 12 determines the whole meaning of Psalm 2. I have adopted H.-J. Kraus's rendering of the text. He follows A. Bertholet, who in 1908 suggested that גילו in verse 11 be placed after נשקו־בר in verse 12. The resulting "original and factually well-founded text . . . [which] also shows consideration for the parallelism of members"[34] is ברעדה נשקו ברגליו.

Whether we emend the text of these verses or whether we leave the text as it stands in the Masoretic Text, and read, "Serve YHWH with fear, and rejoice with trembling. Kiss the son . . . , " the impact of the psalm on its readers/hearers is the same.[35] Indeed, a king of YHWH's choosing once reigned over Israel, and that possibility remains for the future. But for now, in the present circumstances, "serve YHWH with fear."

Psalm 2 is a royal psalm, but in Psalm 2, YHWH sits on the throne. Kingship *is* important, but the enthroned one is YHWH (v. 4). Brevard Childs wonders why this psalm "was placed in such a prominent place unless it was to emphasize the kingship of God as a major theme of the whole Psalter."[36] Childs wonders correctly. To introduce the concept of the kingship of YHWH is precisely the role of Psalm 2 in the Psalter.

We may argue that Psalm 2 points to a future restoration of the Davidic kingship or even beyond that to a future messianic hope. The implications with and ties to David are strong. The postexilic community never gave up hope for a return to the days of a true nation.[37] Zerubbabel was probably one of the victims of the drive to restore the Davidic dynasty in postexilic Israel. And during the late second and early first centuries BCE, the postexilic community launched an ill-fated attempt at

---

[34]Kraus, *Psalms 1–59: A Commentary*, 125. Bertholet's interpretation, of course, disregards *mater lectionis*, the vocalization, and the separation of words. See also Mays, *The Lord Reigns*, 111.

[35]For several treatments of the issue, see A. A. MacIntosh, "A Consideration of the Problems Presented by Psalm ll, 11 and 12," JTS 27 (1976): 1-14; A. Robinson, "Deliberate but Misguided Haplography Explains Psalm 2:11-12," ZAW 89 (1977): 421-22; and William L. Holladay, "A New Proposal for the Crux in Psalm II 12," VT 28 (1978): 110-12.

[36]Childs, *Introduction to the Old Testament as Scripture*, 516.

[37]Hossfeld and Zenger, *Die Psalmen I, Psalm 1–50*, 50-51, agree. They write: Ps 2 "hält daran fest, daß sich JHWH mit der Erwählung 'seines Königs David' ein für allemal daran gebunden hat, seine universale Gottesherrschaft durch ein vom Zion her amtierendes Königtum durchzusetzen ('Davidbund')."

self-government. But for the postexilic community in Jerusalem, the reality of life was as the vassal of a foreign nation, subject to a foreign king.

Psalm 2 closes with "happy are those who take refuge in Him." The אשרי in 2:12 ties Psalm 2 with Psalm 1 as an introduction to the "story" of the Psalter. The pressing need of the postexilic community was identity and stability. Kingship—for ancient Israel, a king of the Davidic line—was the remembered pattern for identity and stability. But postexilic Israel could not have a human king. The means for achieving survival and maintaining identity was to acknowledge YHWH as king (2:11) and to obey YHWH's instruction in the תורה (1:2).

Psalm 3

Psalms 3–41 are a significant collection of Psalms of David. All but two have the superscription לדוד,[38] and most are individual or community laments. Psalm 3 marks the beginning of the collection and should contain, according to the principles of canonical criticism, clues about why it, and the psalms that follow it, were included in the Psalter by the shaping community.

Psalm 3 is a rather "prosaic" composition. It is one of sixty-three psalms in the Psalter that form critics label "individual lament";[39] its superscription contains the customary לדוד;[40] its meter, according to Kraus, is an even double-triple construction;[41] it is brief and presents no major textual problems; the date of its composition, like many of the psalms in the Psalter, is most likely the era of the first Jerusalem temple;

---

[38]Psalm 10 is strongly linked to Psalm 9. See Kraus, *Psalms 1–59: A Commentary*, 188-89, and Holladay, *The Psalms Through Three Thousand Years*, 77. Psalm 33 has solid linguistic links to Psalm 32. See Wilson's treatment in *The Editing of the Hebrew Psalter*, 174-75.

[39]See Bellinger, *Psalms: Reading and Studying the Book of Praises*, 48; Hermann Gunkel, *The Psalms: A Form-Critical Introduction*, trans. Thomas M. Horner, FBBS 19 (Philadelphia: Fortress Press, 1967) 33-35; and Kraus, *Psalms 1–59: A Commentary*, 137. Mowinckel, however, in *The Psalms in Israel's Worship*, 1:219-20, labels Psalm 3 a "protective psalm," since it is a prayer for the protection of YHWH against an imminent danger.

[40]Seventy-four of the psalms in the Hebrew Psalter are ascribed to David. In the Septuagint, eighty-eight psalms are attributed to him. See Holladay, *The Psalms through Three Thousand Years*, 71, 89, for a full discussion.

[41]See Kraus, *Psalms 1–59: A Commentary*, 137.

and its language is conventional and very familiar.[42] What about Psalm 3 appealed to the community that shaped the Psalter and caused them to place it and the thirty-eight psalms that follow it in their positions in the Psalter?

Remember that postexilic ancient Israel was a people struggling to maintain a sense of identity in a world it no longer controlled. James Sanders maintains that postexilic Israel was a people in crisis; they were living in an unstable and significant time in which a decisive change is impending. Sanders suggests that

> in crisis situations, only the old, tried, and true has any real authority. Nothing thought up at the last minute, no matter how clever, can effect the necessary steps of recapitulation and transcendence needed by the threatened community, if it is to survive with identity. A new story will not do; only a story with old, recognizable elements has the power for life required.[43]

What does "crisis" have to do with Psalm 3? A seemingly mundane, "tried and true" psalm like Psalm 3 was just what the threatened second temple community needed to begin its "story" of the reign of David in the Psalter. Just how "tried and true" is it?

Psalm 3 begins with a superscription: "מזמור לדוד when he fled from the presence of Absalom his son." Twelve other psalms in the Psalter locate themselves, in their superscriptions, in particular historical settings in the life of David.[44] Historical superscriptions are viewed generally as late additions to the main texts of the psalms, although discussion continues as to *when* editors added such details.[45]

H.-J. Kraus completely dismisses the value of the superscription for understanding Psalm 3. The psalm has no connection with the event in David's life to which the superscription refers. The psalmist of Psalm 3 "does not flee like David and evinces not a trace of mourning (for Absa-

---

[42]See John S. Kselman, "Psalm 3: A Structural and Literary Study," CBQ 49 (1987): 572.

[43]James A. Sanders, "Adaptable for Life: The Nature and Function of Canon," in *From Sacred Story to Sacred Text* (Philadelphia: Fortress, 1987) 21.

[44]Psalms 7; 18; 34; 51; 52; 54; 56; 57; 59; 60; 63; and 142.

[45]See, e.g., Brevard S. Childs, "Psalm Titles and Midrashic Exegesis," JSS 16 (1971): 137-50; Wilson, *The Editing of the Hebrew Psalter*, 170-72; and Kraus, *Psalms 1–59: A Commentary*, 139.

lom)."[46] Kraus is partially correct. The superscription does not appear to shed any direct light on the meaning of Psalm 3. But James L. Mays suggests an alternative way to consider the historical notes found in the Psalter. He writes:

> David was the sweet psalmist of Israel. The songs that came out of his life as shepherd and warrior, as refugee and ruler, were the inspired expression of a life devoted to God in bad times and good, and therefore the guiding language for all who undertook lives of devotion.[47]

By recalling to mind a specific event in the life of David, the chosen one of YHWH, at the beginning of the Psalter, the superscription immediately directs the attention of the reader/hearer to David and to the "story" they were about to hear.[48]

The following eight verses of Psalm 3 are in the typical form of an individual lament. A lament may be divided into four parts. Part one, the invocation, calls upon YHWH to listen to the psalmist. In part two, the complaint, the psalmist outlines a picture of the distress that occasions the prayer to YHWH. Next comes the petition, which includes the psalmist's rationale for relying on YHWH and the psalmist's specific request of YHWH. Part four, the conclusion, is an expression of confidence in YHWH.[49]

The invocation and the complaint of Psalm 3 are located in verses 2 and 3 (EVV 1 and 2). "O YHWH" is a familiar vocative address, followed by the psalmist's lament about the enemies who are all around. This format is common in the Psalter and is especially prevalent in Book One.[50]

---

[46]Kraus, *Psalm 1–59: A Commentary*, 139. Kraus even ignores the Masoretic Text's practice of designating the superscriptions of the psalms as "verse 1."

[47]James L. Mays, "The David of the Psalms," *Interpretation* 40 (1986): 145.

[48]Childs, *Introduction to the Old Testament as Scripture*, 520-21, suggests that the historical superscriptions served to move the psalms to which they were attached out of their cultic setting and into the history of ancient Israel. While Childs does not go on to draw the conclusion that I suggest, his argument may be used to precisely that end.

[49]Bellinger, *Psalms: Reading and Studying the Book of Praises*, 45-46. Bellinger's model is simplified from his earlier six-part lament, outlined in *Psalmody and Prophecy*, JSOTSup 27 (Sheffield UK: JSOT Press, 1984) 22-24.

[50]See Psalms 22:17; 25:19; 31:14; 38:19; 56:3; 69:5; and 119:157.

Verses 4 through 8 (EVV 3-7) are the petition of the psalm. Verses, 4, 5, 6, and 7, explain the psalmist's rationale for relying on YHWH for deliverance. And verse 8 is the actual petition for help. The picture in verse 4 (3 in EVV) of YHWH as a shield is very prominent in the Psalter, and, like the vocative address found in verse 2, is especially prominent in Book One.[51]

Verse 5 (4 in EVV) can be problematic for interpretation because of its verbal tenses. The verse has אקרא, an imperfect verb, followed by ויענני, an imperfect with vav-consecutive. If we translate the verbs as they appear in the Masoretic Text, the verse reads,

> With my voice I will cry out unto YHWH,
> for He has answered me from His holy mountain.

Many commentators choose to follow the emendation proposed for the second verb by the critical apparatus in BHS and change the vav-consecutive to a simple vav-conjunctive. The verse then reads,

> With my voice I will cry (or, I cry) out unto YHWH,
> and He will answer (or, He answers) me from His holy mountain.[52]

In the journal *Hebrew Studies*, Anson Rainey and a number of other grammarians explore the possibility that the Hebrew verbal system at one time had an additional form—built on the "prefix" or "imperfect" pattern—which was analogous to the Akkadian preterite *iprus*.[53]

---

[51]See Psalms 7:11; 18:3, 31, 36; 28:7; 33:20; 59:12; 84:10, 12; 115:9, 10, 11; 119:114; and 144:2.

[52]See, e.g., Kraus, *Psalms 1–59: A Commentary*, 136-37; Craigie, *Psalms 1–50*, 70-71; and A. A. Anderson, *The Book of Psalms*, vol. 1, 73.

[53]At one time, the narrated past could be expressed in Hebrew by either the affixed "perfect" or by the prefixed "preterite." And the only difference in form in the consonantal text between the prefixed "imperfect" and the prefixed "preterite" was the absence of a final case vowel in the preterite. When final vowels dropped from the Hebrew verbal system, the written form of the preterite became indistinguishable from the written form of the imperfect, although the pronunciation of the two remained distinct. Over the centuries, the affixed perfect form displaced the prefixed preterite as the preferred form for past time, and the pronunciation of the preterite was forgotten. By the time the Masoretes assigned a vocalization to the text of the Hebrew Bible, the preterite was long forgotten, and thus, in many instances when a verb should be understood as a preterite, it is rendered as an imperfect. For a full discussion, see Anson F. Rainey, "The

If we apply the idea of a preterite to the verbs in verse 5 of Psalm 3, we obtain a translation,

> With my voice I cried out unto YHWH,
>   and He answered me from His holy mountain.

Since, in the form of the lament, verse 5 falls within the purview of the psalmist's rationale for relying on YHWH for deliverance, rendering both verbs in past time seems to be the most satisfying option. Thus we may understand אקרא as a preterite and ויענני as a preterite with simple conjunction.

The end of verse 5 contains a significant phrase and ties Psalm 3 to many other psalms in the Psalter. "His holy mountain" is found in, among others, Psalms 2:6; 15:1; 24:3; 48:3 (48:2 in EVV); and 87:1, and is closely paralleled in the Psalter with Zion.[54] The psalmist knows from past experience that YHWH dwells in Zion and that deliverance comes from Zion and from nowhere else.

Verses 6 and 7 (5 and 6 in EVV) continue the psalmist's recital of the rationale for relying on YHWH for deliverance. The verses might indicate that the psalmist is a fugitive who has sought refuge for the night within the temple precincts or that the psalmist is involved in an ordeal procedure that takes place overnight in the temple.[55] The original *Sitz im Leben* of at least this portion of Psalm 3 may well be that of refuge or ordeal, but Peter Craigie's more mundane "location" suits Psalm 3's role in the "story" of the Psalter. Craigie suggests that

> It is [the psalmist's] conviction that "the Lord sustains" that makes sleep possible in an impossible situation. . . . God has sustained him through the night so that now, with the confidence rooted in rest, he could look forward to another day in the presence of a God who "sustains." The

---

Ancient Prefix Conjugation in the Light of Amarnah Canaanite," HS 27 (1986): 4-19; Edward L. Greenstein, "On the Prefixed Preterite in Biblical Hebrew," HS 29 (1988): 7-17; John Huehnergard, "The Early Hebrew Prefix-Conjugations," HS 29 (1988): 19-23; Ziony Zevit, "On Talking Funny in Biblical Henglish and Solving a Problem of the YAQTUL Past Tense," HS 29 (1988): 25-33; and Anson F. Rainey, "Further Remarks on the Hebrew Verbal System," HS 29 (1988): 35-42.

[54]See, e.g., Psalm 2:6.

[55]See K. van der Toorn, "Ordeal Procedures in the Psalms and the Passover Meal," VT 38 (1988): 427-45, for a full discussion.

rest, and its implications, had banished fear, so that those very multitudes which gave rise to the complaint . . . now cause no fear.[56]

The psalmist shares a common human experience, expressed in the adage "It is always darkest before the dawn." Troubles never seem so overwhelming in the light of day as they do in the dark of night.

In verse 6, the prefixed form יסמכני (he will sustain me) may be translated in a traditional imperfect sense because this verb serves, along with verse 7 (which also contains an imperfect verb), as the tie between the psalmist's rationale for relying on YHWH for deliverance and the actual petition that follows in verse 8. "I awoke for I know that YHWH will sustain me, and I will not fear. . . . "

In verse 8 (7 in EVV) we read the psalmist's petition, the request for help. We encounter here for the third time in Psalm 3 the familiar vocative address, "O YHWH." It is as though the psalmist wants to be very sure that YHWH is paying attention and heeding the lament. And the psalmist uses a conventional—and perhaps tried and true—phrase to encourage YHWH to action. "Rise up, O YHWH" occurs numerous times in Book One[57] and in many places throughout the remainder of the Psalter.

The psalmist then suggests a method by which YHWH might effect deliverance. The language of verse 8 (EVV 7) indicates that the psalmist bases the petition upon a remembered deliverance at the hands of YHWH:

For you have struck all my enemies on the jaw,
the teeth of the wicked you have shattered."[58]

In the laments of the Psalter, the psalmists frequently refer to the speech organs—the mouth, throat, tongue, lips, and teeth—of their enemies as sources of trouble and as targets for punishment.[59]

---

[56]Craigie, *Psalms 1–50*, 74.

[57]See Psalms 7:7 (7:6 in EVV); 9:20 (9:19 in EVV); 10:12; 17:13; and 35:2.

[58]See Kraus, *Psalms 1–59: A Commentary*, 141. My translation of the two perfects as past time is in opposition to Craigie who, following Mitchell Dahood (*Psalms 1–50*. AB 16 [Garden City NY: Doubleday, 1966] 19-21), translates them in a jussive sense. See Craigie, *Psalms 1–50*, 74-75.

[59]See Psalms 5:10 (5:9 in EVV); 10:7; 31:19 (31:18 in EVV); 52:4 (52:2 in EVV); 57:5 (57:4 in EVV); 58:7 (58:6 in EVV); 59:8 (59:7 in EVV); 140:4 (140:3 in EVV).

Verse 9 is the conclusion to the individual lament of Psalm 3.[60]
Again, we encounter commonplace language. References to YHWH's
blessing and deliverance occur throughout the Psalter.[61]

Book One of the Psalter is a magnificent collection of Psalms of
David. And Psalm 3 is an ideal "beginning" for the collection. The psalm
is certainly guilty of all accusations levelled against it. It is brief; it is, in
form, a predictable lament; its language is prosaic; and copyists and
translators have not quarreled much over its meaning and intent. Psalm
3 is comfortable.

But it is powerful. Like any good introduction, Psalm 3 introduces its
hearers to the subject matter of Book One. Using the paradigm of the life
of David, YHWH's chosen king, the psalm begins in distress and lament
(vv. 2, 3). Enemies are all around and are talking together about—conspiring against (?)—the psalmist.[62] The psalm moves in verses 4-7 to a
lengthy rationale for relying on YHWH to protect and sustain. The psalmist reiterates again and again that YHWH is the source of strength. The last
two verses of Psalm 3 express a sure confidence that YHWH will "strike
down" the enemies and place divine "blessing" upon the faithful psalmist.

Is not the "story" of Psalm 3 the "story" of David as we encounter
him in the Deuteronomistic History? And is it not the story—the "drama
in miniature"—of the Psalter? Ancient Israel had once been a powerful
nation under the leadership of David. But dark days descended, and
Babylon carried the people away into exile. The people are back in their
own land now, but enemies are all around. They have only to rely on
YHWH as they did in the past—and as David did—and YHWH will "strike
down" their enemies and bless ancient Israel once again.

---

[60]Kraus maintains that verse 9 is a closing statement, or "epiphonema," added
to the psalm for liturgical purposes. See Kraus, *Psalms 1–59: A Commentary*,
141-42. He may be correct, but since we are examining the role of Psalm 3
within the Psalter, we will treat verse 9 as an integral part of the psalm and as
a necessary conclusion to the psalmist's lament.

[61]See Psalms 24:6 (24:5 in EVV); 27:1; 28:8, 9; 29:11; 35:3; 62:8 (62:7 in
EVV); 109:26; 118:14.

[62]As we also see in Psalm 2:2. See John Eaton, *Kingship and the Psalms*,
2nd ed. (Sheffield: JSOT Press, 1986) 27-29. Eaton maintains that the psalm
"expresses clearly and directly the situation of an embattled king." And he
argues, thus, that Psalm 3 is a "royal" psalm. Eaton, however, classifies the
majority of the psalms in the Psalter as "royal."

What a powerful message to postexilic Israel and what a powerful beginning for Book One of the Psalter! But the message is made even more powerful by the orthodoxy of the medium. When the shaping community heard Psalm 3, the words were familiar. Phrase after phrase of the psalm brought to mind other psalms, other pieces of ancient Israel's tradition.[63] And the words reminded the people that they had a long-standing and powerful relationship with their God. Psalm 3, then, fits the definition of a vehicle of stability and identity during a time of crisis. It is, indeed, "old, tried, and true." But its canonical position as part of the Hebrew Psalter gives this old, tried, and true psalm a new meaning and a new function for its postexilic audience. The psalm brings to mind king David, but it pushes its hearers beyond David to the new realities of postexilic life.

Psalm 41

Book One of the Psalter closes with Psalm 41, a psalm of David that expresses great self-assurance that YHWH is gracious to and pleased with the psalmist and that the psalmist will be stationed in the presence of YHWH forever. Psalm 41 is just another of Book One's "psalms of David," but it is interesting in that it begins with אשרי, the same word with which Psalm 1 begins and Psalm 2 ends. And while Psalm 41 opens in verses 2-4 (1-3 in EVV) in the third person, the remainder of it is in the first person. What can these two features tell us about how the shaping community appropriated this psalm into the story of the Psalter?

Sigmund Mowinckel and Peter Craigie characterize the psalm as a "psalm of illness."[64] Craigie maintains that the original *Sitz im Leben* of the psalm is as the liturgy used in a ritual in which a sick person comes to the temple to find healing. He outlines the contents of the psalm in the following manner: verses 2-4 (1-3 in EVV) are the words spoken by the priest of the temple to the sick person; verses 5-11 (4-10 in EVV) are the sick person's lament; between verses 11 and 12 (10 and 11 in EVV) is an

---

[63]One "piece of tradition" in Psalm 3 that will be significant later in my discussion of Psalm 90 is the repeated use of ישע (vv. 3, 8, 9), which reminds the reader/hearer of Moses's speech in Exodus 15. Verse 2 says: "YHWH is my strength and song. He has become my salvation (ויהי־לי לישועה)."

[64]Mowinckel, *The Psalms in Israel's Worship*, 2:9; and Craigie, *Psalms 1-50*, 319.

unrecorded oracle from YHWH concerning healing for the sick person; and verses 12-14 (11-13 in EVV) are the sick person's expression of confidence in YHWH's graciousness.[65]

H.-J. Kraus and Hossfeld and Zenger call Psalm 41 a prayer song. Their analyses of the psalm are less structured than Craigie's, but they give the psalm a more general location in the life of ancient Israel. Verses 2-4 are didactic in character, a general opening for the psalm in the third person; verses 5-11 are a prayer for relief from distress; and verses 12-14 are a song of thanksgiving.[66]

While both Craigie's and Kraus's analyses provide plausible explanations for the change in voice from third to first person at verse 5, the switch *is* abrupt and verses 2-4 seem somewhat out of place in this otherwise simple psalm of lament. Another explanation is that the community which shaped the Psalter added verses 2-4—an existing blessing in the third person—to the beginning of the first-person psalm to tie Book One securely with Psalms 1 and 2. These verses are, then, another "footprint" of the shaping community. The end of Book One brings the reader/hearer back to the Torah, the instruction, at the beginning of the Psalter: "Happy is the one who trusts in YHWH."[67]

Psalm 41 is a fitting conclusion to the laments of David collected in Book One, and the community that shaped the Psalter formed Psalm 41 into a fitting conclusion to the opening of the Psalter. Blessed is the one who remembers YHWH and YHWH's Torah and is sure of YHWH's protection despite the ongoing presence of enemies.

> By this I know that you are pleased with me,
>   Because my enemy does not shout in triumph over me.
> As for me, you uphold me in my integrity,
>   And you set me in your presence forever. (vv. 12, 13; EVV 11, 12)

---

[65]Craigie, *Psalms 1–50*, 319.

[66]Kraus, *Psalms 1–59: A Commentary*, 430. Hossfeld and Zenger, *Die Psalmen I, Psalm 1–50*, 257-59, write, however, that "in the core of the psalm lies hidden an old, preexilic lament-prayer of a persecuted sick person (vv. 5-11 [4-10 in EVV])."

[67]Kraus certainly allows the possibility when he writes, "Psalm 41 has a long road of tradition behind it in which it was reconstructed and newly formed. . . . What we have here is probably a prayer song that is to be dated as relatively late." See Kraus, *Psalms 1–59: A Commentary*, 431.

Chapter 6

Kingship
in the Ancient Near East

An exploration of the concept of kingship in the ancient Near East will be helpful in understanding the importance of kingship for the postexilic community. The exilic and postexilic Israelite communities looked back to the time of David and Solomon as a "golden era." Robert Coote and Keith Whitelam, in *The Emergence of Early Israel In Historical Perspective*, maintain, in fact, that the formation of the Davidic state was "crucial in shaping and defining the nature and identity of Israel as it is presented in the Bible."[1] What was so significant about kingship?

Kingship *was* a highly successful form of government—of order and structure—in the ancient Near East. In fact, we may say that kingship was the *only* form of government in the ancient Near East. Kings were able to centralize societies around single frames of reference—courts and temples—and often managed to achieve political unity among peoples of great ancestral diversity.

Scribes in both Egypt and Mesopotamia recorded stories of the origins of kingship in their societies. The stories tell us that kingship was instituted at specific points in time in the history of the cultures. And it was instituted to meet certain needs. According to records from ancient Egypt, kingship "evolved" there at a crucial time in its history. In the early phases of the Gerzean period (from 3500 BCE), Egyptian culture developed a high degree of craft specialization, long-distance trade within Egypt, and sustained contacts with southwestern Asia. New social and

---

[1] Robert B. Coote and Keith W. Whitelam, *The Emergence of Early Israel in Historical Perspective* (Sheffield: Almond Press, 1987) 169.

economic circumstances encouraged and in many ways required the development of a hierarchical society.

Egyptian myth tells us that kingship originated in the realm of the gods. The Memphite Theology dates to the time of the Old Kingdom (third millennium BCE).[2] The text is a treatise, sometimes read as a dramatic play, which gives the reader/hearer a rationale for the institution of kingship in Egypt and its relationship to the gods and to society.

According to the Memphite Theology, Ptah is the supreme god and creator of the world and great king over all Egypt. Ptah, however, empowers Geb, the "lord of the Gods," to appoint two kings, one to rule Upper Egypt and one to rule Lower Egypt. Geb chooses the gods Seth and Horus to rule the two parts of Egypt:

> Thus Horus stood over one region, and Seth stood over one region. They made peace over the Two Lands at Ayan. That was the division of the Two Lands. ·
> Geb's words to Horus and Seth: "I have separated you."—Lower and Upper Egypt.[3]

After the appointments, Geb reconsiders his decision and decides Egypt should be united under a single king. He appoints Horus as ruler of both Upper and Lower Egypt.

> Then Horus stood over the land. He is the uniter of this land, proclaimed in the great name: Ta-tenen, South-of-his-Wall, Lord of Eternity. Then sprouted the two Great Magicians upon his head. He is Horus who arose as king of Upper and Lower Egypt, who united the Two Lands in the Nome of the Wall, the place in which the Two Lands were united.[4]

Horus, as a direct descendant of Ptah, is now king of a united Egyptian kingdom. Miriam Lichtheim suggests that the Memphite

---

[2]Miriam Lichtheim, *Ancient Egyptian Literature*, vol. 1 (Berkeley: University of California Press, 1973) 51, writes that the language of the Memphite Theology is archaic and resembles that of the Pyramid Texts.

[3]Ibid., 52. See also James B. Pritchard, ed., *Ancient Near Eastern Texts Relating to the Old Testament*, 3rd ed. (Princeton: Princeton University Press, 1969) 4-6.

[4]Lichtheim, *Ancient Egyptian Literature*, 1:53. Pritchard, *Ancient Near Eastern Texts Relating to the Old Testament*, 4-5.

Theology blends two traditions, two memories, about the origin of kingship in ancient Egypt. One memory is of the land divided into two kingdoms, Upper Egypt and Lower Egypt. Reflecting that memory, the Memphite Theology states that Geb appoints Horus and Seth as rulers of a divided land. Another memory is that Egypt was always a united land. And so, in the end, Geb declares Horus as the sole ruler. While readers/hearers may understand the origins of the story in different ways, the message of the story is clear: the gods are the supreme powers in the world; the Egyptian kings are descended from the gods; and the kings are given their thrones *by the gods*.[5]

The Building Inscription of Sesostris I, who reigned during the Twelfth Dynasty, also known as the Berlin Leather Roll, contains a lengthy rationale for the legitimacy of the king in Egyptian culture. It confirms the affirmation of the Memphite Theology about the origins of kingship in Egypt. The king is the offspring of the gods, appointed—destined—to rule before the beginning of life. Sesostris declares:

> He (Horus) begat me to do what should be done for him,
>   to accomplish what he commands to do.
> He appointed me shepherd of this land,
>   knowing him who would herd it for him.
> . . .
> I am king by nature,
>   ruler to whom one does not give.
> I conquered as a fledgling,
>   I lorded in the egg,
> I ruled as a youth.
>   He advanced me to Lord of the Two Parts,
>   a child yet wearing swaddling clothes.
> He destined me to rule the people,
>   made me to be before humankind.[6]

The purpose of many of the Egyptian royal texts is to relate the person of the living king in the closest possible way to royal ancestors so that royal succession was wrapped up in a "central and authoritative

---

[5]Lichtheim, *Ancient Egyptian Literature*, 1:116.
[6]Ibid., 116.

collection of myth."[7] Thus, kingship is legitimated by connecting both the office and the person of the king with the divine realm.

Mesopotamian myth tells us that the most ancient political institution in the ancient Near East was an assembly of all free people which elected, in times of emergency—foreign threat, economic hardship, or natural disaster—a leader to take charge of responding to the crisis. When the emergency was past, the elected leader relinquished the powers to the assembly. Sometime during the third millennium BCE, communities in the Tigris-Euphrates valley grew steadily in size and number until general assemblies and temporary leaders were no longer sufficient to administer the daily affairs of the burgeoning communities.[8]

Enuma Elish, an epic composed sometime in the early second millennium, tells the story of the evolution of kingship among the ancient Babylonian gods. The story deals with the origins of the basic powers in the universe, and explains how the present world order came to be established.[9] We learn in the epic's first section that the gods governed themselves through a large assembly made up of all the gods. In times of emergency, the assembly granted kingship to one of their number who took charge of the situation and carried out appropriate actions.

In the second section of the epic, Tiamat, the goddess of the sea waters, creates an army of monster serpents and roaring dragons to avenge an old grudge against the other gods.[10] The gods are understandably disturbed by Tiamat's threat and gather in their assembly to invest young Marduk, the son of Ea and grandson of Anu, with the task of defeating the angry Tiamat.

---

[7]Barry J. Kemp, "Old Kingdom, Middle Kingdom and Second Intermediate Period," in *Ancient Egypt: A Social History*, ed. B. G. Trigger, B. J. Kemp, D. O'Connor, and A. B. Lloyd (Cambridge: Cambridge University Press, 1983) 73.

[8]Henri Frankfort, *Kingship and the Gods* (Chicago: University of Chicago Press, 1948, 1978) 215 and 218-19.

[9]Thorkild Jacobsen, *Treasures of Darkness* (New Haven CT: Yale University Press, 1976) 168.

[10]Pritchard, *Ancient Near Eastern Texts Relating to the Old Testament*, 63, tablet II, lines 1-26; and W. G. Lambert and Simon B. Parker, eds., *Enūma Eliš: The Babylonian Epic of Creation, The Cuneiform Text* (Oxford: Clarendon Press, 1966).

Joyfully they did homage: "Marduk is king!"
They conferred on him scepter, throne, and vestment;
They gave him matchless weapons that ward off the foes:
"Go and cut off the life of Tiamat.
May the winds bear her blood to places undisclosed."[11]

Marduk boldly goes to war against Tiamat and her army of monsters and defeats them soundly. He returns triumphantly to the assembly of the gods, is seated on a throne, and given homage by them. The gods then confer on him a new title:

"His name shall be 'king of the gods of heaven and underworld'
      [*LUGAL-DIMMER-ANKIA*], trust in him!"
When they had given the sovereignty to Marduk,
They declared for him good fortune and success:
"Henceforth thou wilt be the patron of our sanctuaries,
Whatever thou dost command we will do."[12]

---

[11]Pritchard, *Ancient Near Eastern Texts Relating to the Old Testament*, 66, tablet IV, lines 28-32. This is E. A. Speiser's translation. Stephanie Dalley, in *Myths from Mesopotamia: Creation, The Flood, Gilgamesh, and Others* (Oxford: Oxford University Press, 1989) 250, translates the passage as:

They rejoiced, they proclaimed: "Marduk is King!"
They invested him with sceptre, throne, and staff-of-office.
They gave him an unfaceable weapon to crush the foe.
      "Go, and cut off the life of Tiamat!
      Let the winds bear her blood to us as good news!"

[12]Pritchard, *Ancient Near Eastern Texts Relating to the Old Testament*, 502, tablet V, lines 112-16. A. K. Grayson, who provides the translation for this portion of *Enuma Elish* in ANET, translates LUGAL-DIMMER-ANKIA as "king of the gods of heaven and the underworld" based on tablet VI, line 142, which reads, "LUGAL-DIMMER-ANKIA is his name which we proclaimed in our assembly. His commands we have exalted above the gods, his fathers. Verily, he is lord of all the gods of heaven and the underworld." Dalley, in *Myths from Mesopotamia*, 259, translates the passage as:

"LUGAL-DIMMER-ANKIA is his name. Trust in him!"
When they gave kingship to Marduk,
They spoke an oration for him, for blessing and obedience.
"Henceforth you shall be the provider of shrines for us.
Whatever you command, we shall perform."

Marduk is now the permanent king of the gods. He builds for himself a city, Babylon, and creates humankind to serve him there.

Thorkild Jacobsen characterizes *Enuma Elish* as a "mythopoeic adumbration" of Babylon's and Marduk's rise to rulership over Babylon which has been projected back into mythical times and made universal in scope. It is an account of how kingship evolved and gained acceptance.[13] Kingship originated among the gods, not as a natural part of the world order, but as the outcome of a threat to their well-being and security.

For the Mesopotamians, kingship had not been a part of the original cosmic order, but came about as the result of a specific event—Marduk's defeat of Tiamat and his ratification by the assembly of the gods as "king of the gods of heaven and underworld."[14] In the same way, kingship had not always been a part of the human world order. It originated in the realm of the gods and was given to humankind by them.

According to Mesopotamian thought, in the earliest times, and again after the Great Flood, "kingship descended from heaven." *The Sumerian King List*, composed during the late third millennium, begins with these words:

> When kingship [*LUGAL*] was lowered from heaven [*an-ta*], kingship [*LUGAL*] was first in Eridu. In Eridu, Alulim became king [*LUGAL*] and ruled [*ì-a*] 28,800 years. . . .[15]

A long list of pre-Flood rulers and the lengths of their reigns follows. Then we read:

> After the Flood had swept over (the earth) (and)
> when kingship [*LUGAL*] was lowered (again) from heaven [*an-ta*],
> kingship [*LUGAL*] was in Kish.[16]

---

[13]Jacobsen, *The Treasures of Darkness*, 191.

[14]Pritchard, *Ancient Near Eastern Texts Relating to the Old Testament*, 502, tablet V, line 112.

[15]Ibid., 265, and Thorkild Jacobsen, *The Sumerian King List*, Assyrian Studies 11 (Chicago: University of Chicago Press, 1939) 70-71.

[16]Pritchard, *Ancient Near East Texts Relating to the Old Testament*, 265, and Jacobsen, *The Sumerian King List*, 76-77.

The Legend of Etana, from the early second millennium, details how this kingship was lowered to the city of Kish and placed upon the shepherd Etana.

> The Igigi, in all, had not set up a king.
> At that time, no tiara had been tied on, nor crown,
> And no scepter had been inlaid with lapis;
>
> . . .
>
> Scepter, crown, tiara, and crook
> Lay deposited before Anu in heaven,
> There being no counseling [*mitluku*] for its people.
> (Then) kingship descended from heaven.[17]

Henri Frankfort calls the phrase "kingship descended from heaven" a "remarkable formula" and suggests that it "combines the awareness that kingship had not always existed with the fact that it represented the only known form of government in historical times."[18]

The prologue to the law code of Hammurapi, the eighteenth century king of Babylon, describes how Marduk, the god of Babylon, entrusted Hammurapi with the administration of the city.

> When lofty Anum, king of the Anunnaki,
> (and) Enlil, lord of heaven and earth,
> the determiner of the destinies of the land,
> determined for Marduk, the firstborn of Enki,
> the Enlil functions over all mankind,
> made him great among the Igigi,
> called Babylon by its exalted name,
> made it supreme in the world,

---

[17]Pritchard, *Ancient Near Eastern Texts Relating to the Old Testament*, 114, lines 6-14. Dalley, *Myths from Mesopotamia*, 190, translates the lines as:

> They (the Igigi) had not established a king over all the teeming people.
> At that time the headband and crown had not been put together,
> And the lapis lazuli sceptre had not been brandished,
>
> . . .
>
> [from the Old Babylonian Version] Sceptre and crown, headband and staffs,
> Were set before Anum in heaven.
> There was no advice for its people,
> (Until) kingship came down from heaven.

[18]Frankfort, *Kingship and the Gods*, 237.

established for him in its midst an enduring kingship
  [*sar-ru-tam da-ri-tam*]
whose foundations are as firm as heaven and earth—
at that time Anum and Enlil named me
to make good the flesh of the people,
me Hammurapi, the devout, god-fearing prince.[19]

Kingship, then, originated in the divine realm, was given to humankind
by the gods, and was sanctioned by them as a means of establishing
order on the earth.

In the early first millennium BCE, a scribe composed a lament for the
city of Ur, which had been destroyed by the Elamites. In *The Lament
Over the Destruction of Sumer and Ur*, we read that the Sumerian gods
An, Enlil, Enki, and Ninhursag decree a tragic fate for the magnificent
city:

That the day be overturned, that "law and order" cease to exist . . .
That the home of kingship [*nam-lugal*] be changed,
That kingship be carried off from the land,
That its face be directed to inimical soil,
That in accord with the command of An (and) Enlil,
  "law and order" cease to exist.[20]

The gods removed kingship from the city of Ur. Chaos and destruction
resulted.

According to the ancient Egyptian and Mesopotamian myths, the
institution of kingship had been given by the gods, was administered by

---

[19]Pritchard, *Ancient Near Eastern Texts Relating to the Old Testament*, 164,
lines 7-30; and A. Deimel, *Codex Hammurabi* (Rome: Pontifical Biblical
Institute, 1950) 2.

[20]Pritchard, ANET, 612, lines 1, 17-22. Piotr Michalowski, in *The Lamentation Over the Destruction of Sumer and Ur* (Winona Lake IN: Eisenbrauns,
1989) 36-37, translates the lines as:

To overturn the (appointed) time, to forsake the (preordained) plans,
To change the location of kingship,
To defile the rights and decrees,
To take away kingship from the land,
To cast the eye (of the storm) on all the land,
To forsake the divine decrees by the order of An and Enlil,
After An had frowned upon all the lands. . . .

divinely appointed monarchs, and was the guarantee of an orderly, lawful pattern of life.[21] The king's function in the world was to give protection against enemies, external and internal, and to insure the reign of justice and righteousness in human affairs.

While caution must always be used when drawing parallels between one ancient Near Eastern society and another, the ancient Egyptian and Mesopotamian views of "king" and "kingship" provide valuable insights into the attitude of ancient Israel toward its own monarchy. Once the group we identify as the "ancient Israelites" settled in communities in the central regions of Palestine, they developed a societal structure that demanded centralization of leadership.[22] The causes for and processes by which this structuring took place were complex, but Israel followed a pattern that was common in communities in the ancient Near East.

During the twelfth and eleventh centuries BCE, the Israelites occupied a number of small settlements in the central highlands of Palestine. The settlements grew quickly in response to a number of social, political, and economic events taking place at the time in the ancient Near East: trade increased; Egypt reemerged as a major power; and Phoenicia, Edom, Ammon, and Syria became regional trade and political centers. As the settlements grew and the surrounding environment changed, the people needed centralized leadership and organization in order to survive and grow.

By the end of the eleventh century BCE, regional Israelite leaders, whose campaigns against their enemies are described in legendary fashion in the Book of Judges, were no longer adequate to manage the social, political, and economic entity we call ancient Israel. Samuel anoints Saul as the permanent king of the ancient Israelites:

> Then Samuel took the flask of oil, poured it on his head, kissed him and said, "Has not YHWH anointed you a ruler (נגיד) over His inheritance?" (1 Samuel 10:1)

---

[21]The monarch was an actual descendant of the gods in Egypt. In Mesopotamia, the monarch was a divinely appointed human overseer.

[22]Gösta Ahlström maintains that the natural form of political and economic centralization in the ancient Near East was the state with a monarch at its head. See *The History of Ancient Palestine* (Minneapolis: Fortress Press, 1993) 334.

According to the Deuteronomistic History, Saul spent most of his reign
in war against the Philistines. He performed the kingly duties for which
the people had requested him of Samuel:

> . . . there shall be a king (מלך) over us, that we also may be like the
> nations, that our king may judge us and go out before us and fight our
> battles. (1 Samuel 8:18b-19)

The balance of the Deuteronomistic History focuses almost exclusively
on the origin, growth, and events in the lives of the Israelite monarchy
through half a millennium of history. Ancient Israel followed a natural
pattern in the ancient Near East. It developed into a society which
required centralization of power in king, court, and temple. And it
developed a "story of kingship" which assured the position of the
monarchy within society. According to the Deuteronomistic History,
YHWH appointed a king over ancient Israel and assured the continuance
of the royal lineage.

In the postexilic period, ancient Israel's temple and cult were
restored, but king and court were not. The history of early Judaism and
the formation of the Hebrew scriptures is the story of the people's
attempts to deal with the loss of these centralizing elements of their
society. The royal psalms in general, and Psalm 2 in particular, address
the postexilic community's questions about this loss. The issue is central
to the canonical shaping of the Psalter.

Chapter 7

Book Two

Psalm 42

Book Two of the Psalter opens with a collection of Psalms of the Sons of Qorah (Psalms 42–49, 84–85, and 87–88) and marks the beginning of what critics call the Elohistic Psalter (Psalms 42–83). Like Book One, Book Two consists mainly of individual and community laments. So while Book One's collection of laments closes with a note of optimism in Psalm 41, the causes of lamenting are still present. Psalm 42 at the beginning of Book Two continues the lament begun in Book One. Unlike Book One, however, only eighteen of Book Two's thirty-one psalms are attributed to David. The focus is still the Davidic dynasty, but David is not as prominent in Book Two.

Psalm 42 is "a Maskil of the Sons of Qorah." The sons of Qorah are closely associated with David and Solomon in the Chronicler's History. First Chronicles 9:19 states that "the Qorahites were over the work of the service, keepers of the thresholds of the tent; and their fathers had been over the camp of YHWH, keepers of the entrance." 1 Chronicles 6:31-38 tells us:

> Now these are those whom David appointed over the service of song in the house of YHWH, after the ark rested there. And they ministered with song before the tabernacle of the tent of meeting, until Solomon had built the house of YHWH in Jerusalem; and they stood over their office according to their order. And these are those who stood with their sons. From the sons of the Kohathites were Heman the singer . . . the son of Qorah, the son of Izhar, the son of Kohath, the son of Levi, the son of Israel.

The Qorahites are listed in Numbers 26:58 as one of the five major Levitical families, but in other places they appear as a subgroup of the

Kohathites.[1] Numbers 16 relates a dramatic incident in which Qorah, along with Dathan and Abiram, questions Moses's and Aaron's authority over the people of Israel. This narrative appears to have served as the rationale for separating the levitical priests into two groups—those who could trace their lineage directly through Aaron—and through Zadok, according to Ezekiel[2]—and those who were descendants of Levi through other sons. The Aaronic priests performed the major sacrificial and cultic duties at the Jerusalem temple, while the Qorahites were doorkeepers and singers and performed the more menial chores.

As singers at the temple, the Qorahites would have been part of the group responsible for the collection, preservation, and shaping of the cultic songs of Israel which became the Psalter. And as we observed in chapter 3, they would perhaps have been a little closer to the common people than the Aaronic priests and thus understood and reflected the hermeneutical underpinnings held by the postexilic community.[3]

Psalm 42 is an individual lament in two sections, verses 2-5 (1-4 in EVV) and verses 7-11 (6-10 in EVV), each followed by the refrain:

> Why are you bowed down, my נפשׁ (being)
> And become disturbed within me?
> Wait for God, for yet I will praise him
> For the help of his presence.[4]

Because Psalm 43 has the same refrain as Psalm 42, many argue that the two psalms belong together as a unit.[5] The Masoretic Text separates the

---

[1]See Exodus 6:18-21; and 1 Chronicles 6:22-24, 31-38. In each of these listings, the Qorahites are listed in third position, always after the Kohathites.

[2]See Ezekiel 44:10-16.

[3]Michael Goulder argues that the Psalms of Qorah originated in the northern kingdom and were brought south and appropriated for use in the Jerusalem cult. For a complete treatment of the issues, see *The Psalms of the Sons of Korah*, JSOTSup 20 (Sheffield UK: JSOT Press, 1982).

[4]The refrains in verse 12 (11 in EVV) and in 43:5 end, "the help of my countenance and my God." Changing 42:6 to conform to the other two refrains would require making the first word of verse 7 the last word of verse 6 and changing the word divisions. Thus פני אלהי would become פני ואלהי.

[5]See, e.g., H.-J. Kraus, *Psalms 1–59: A Commentary*, trans. H. C. Oswald (Minneapolis: Augsburg Publishing House, 1988) 435-42; Peter C. Craigie, *Psalms 1–50*, WBC 19 (Waco TX: Word Books, 1985 323-29; Gerald H. Wilson, *The Editing of the Hebrew Psalter*, SBLDS 76 (Chico CA: Scholars

two, but Kennicott lists thirty-nine manuscripts which join Psalms 42 and 43.[6] Interestingly, the Septuagint separates the psalms and gives Psalm 43 a distinct title, "A Psalm of David." The refrain certainly provides justification for considering the two psalms together, but in Psalm 42 the psalmist is speaking to self, to נפשׁ, and in Psalm 43 the psalmist is speaking to God. The common refrain may have prompted the collectors of the Qorahite songs to place these similar psalms side by side, but it does not necessarily indicate that they were at one time a single psalm.

The psalmist is in dialogue with self—the נפשׁ.[7] In this regard, Psalm 42 may be likened to the Egyptian tale "The Dispute between a Man and His Ba." Miriam Lichtheim, in *Ancient Egyptian Literature*, summarizes the tale:

> A man who suffers from life longs for death. Angered by his complaints, his *ba* threatens to leave him. This threat fills the man with horror, for to be abandoned by his *ba* would mean total annihilation, instead of the resurrection and immortal bliss that he envisages. He therefore implores his *ba* to remain with him, and not to oppose him in his longing for death.[8]

In Psalm 42, the psalmist persuades the נפשׁ not to despair, since the psalmist is convinced that YHWH is still a source of help.

Verses 2-5 (1-4 in EVV) and 7-11 (6-10 in EVV) of Psalm 42 use powerful images of water to express the psalmist's need for YHWH and the feeling of removal from YHWH's presence. Verses 2-5 are nostalgic, lamenting that life is no longer as it used to be. Thus the psalmist thirsts (צמא) after brooks of water (אפיקי־מים), cries tears (דמע), and pours out (שׁפך) the נפשׁ to God.

Press, 1985) 176-77; and Frank-Lothar Hossfeld and Erich Zenger, *Die Psalmen I, Psalm 1–50*, NEchtB (Würzburg: Echter Verlag, 1993) 265.

[6]Wilson, *The Editing of the Hebrew Psalter*, 176.

[7]Luis Alonso Schökel suggests that the inner dialogue is the expression of an "inner drama" in which the psalmist and the psalmist's self argue about their current standing in relationship to God. See "The Poetic Structure of Psalm 42–43," JSOT 1 (1976): 8.

[8]Miriam Lichtheim, *Ancient Egyptian Literature*, vol. 1 (Berkeley: University of California Press, 1973) 163-69; and James B. Pritchard, ed. *Ancient Near Eastern Texts Relating to the Old Testament*, 3rd. ed. (Princeton: Princeton University Press, 1969) 405-407.

For I used to go along with the throng
    and lead them unto the house of God.
With the voice of joy and thanksgiving,
    a multitude keeping festival. (v. 5; EVV 4)

Verses 7-11 use water images to express distress and despair over present circumstances. The psalmist despairs at feelings of being overcome by the deep (תהום), by waterfalls (צנורים), by breakers (משברים), and by waves (גלים).[9]

O my God, my נפש is bowed down within me . . .
    Deep calls to deep at the voice of Your waterfalls;
All Your breakers and Your waves have rolled over me.
                               (vv. 7, 8; EVV 6, 7)

    The taunts of the psalmist's enemies and adversaries in verses 4 and 11 (3 and 10 in EVV) serve to heighten the psalmist's sense of God's absence and the psalmist's nostalgia.[10]

My tears have been to me food day and night,
    While they are saying to me,
    "Where is your God?" (v. 4)

Like a shattering of my bones,
    my adversaries revile me,
While they are saying all day,
    "Where is your God?" (v. 11)

Thus God's absence is felt all the more because of the constant reminders given by the psalmist's enemies that God is not "here," is not present. But before feelings of despair completely consume the psalmist, the refrain calls the נפש back from its musings.

    The refrains reflect the psalmist's confidence and hope that God is present, even in apparently difficult circumstances. The words זכר "remember" and יחל "wait" occur repeatedly in Psalm 42. Verses 5 and 7 (4 and 6 in EVV) stress the nostalgic remembrance of God. Verse 10 (9

---

    [9]Schökel, "The Poetic Structure of Psalm 42–43," 4.
    [10]Sarcastic, taunting questions are often found on the lips of enemies in the Psalter and elsewhere in the Hebrew scriptures. See Psalms 79:10; 115:2; Joel 2:17; and Micah 7:10.

in EVV) admonishes God not to forget the psalmist. And verses 6 and 12 (5 and 11 in EVV) admonish the נפש to wait for God.

Imagine the impact of Psalm 42 on the postexilic reader/hearer. The postexilic community is a people attempting to retain their identity and a sense of stability by finding answers to the questions "Who are we?" and "What are we to do?" The psalmist no longer participates in the festivals at the house of God, but instead thirsts for God and argues within the self about hope and despair. The remembered past of ancient Israel, the "Who are we?", is a story of despair—removal from the house of God—and nostalgia—thirsting after the past. But the despair in the story must be tempered with remembrance and anticipation. "Wait for God, you shall again praise Him," and you shall experience God's presence. The community that shaped the Psalter placed the collection of psalms beginning with Psalm 42 in its position in the Psalter to remind the readers/hearers that within their present despair is the hope found in YHWH.[11]

Psalm 72

Book Two concludes with Psalm 72, a royal psalm, but only one of two psalms in the Psalter ascribed to Solomon. H.-J. Kraus characterizes it as a collection of wishes and prayers for the well-being of the king, probably preexilic in origin, and possibly used at an enthronement festival in Jerusalem.[12]

Gerald Wilson views Psalm 72 as one of the Psalter's strategically placed royal psalms. He maintains that the psalm functions in the story of the Psalter as David's "attempt to transfer the blessings of his covenant with YHWH to his descendants."[13]

Brevard Childs writes that the canonical placement of Psalm 72 indicates strongly that the psalm "is 'for' Solomon, offered by David."[14] It

[11]J. Clinton McCann, Jr., "Books I–III and the Editorial Purpose of the Psalter," in *The Shape and Shaping of the Psalter*, JSOTSup 159 (Sheffield UK: JSOT Press, 1993) 95, argues that the placement of the communal lament Psalms 44 and 74 after the introductory psalms of Books Two and Three serve as "instruction to an exilic community not only to face the disorienting reality of exile but also to reach toward a reorientation beyond the traditional grounds for hope, that is, beyond the Davidic/Zion covenant theology."

[12]Kraus, *Psalms 60–150: A Commentary*, 76-77.

[13]Gerald H. Wilson, "The Use of Royal Psalms at the 'Seams' of the Psalter," JSOT 35 (1986): 89.

[14]Brevard S. Childs, *Introduction to the Old Testament as Scripture*

brings to the minds of its readers/hearers the covenant that YHWH made with David in 2 Samuel, chapter 7, and which YHWH renewed with Solomon in 1 Kings 9:5:

> I will establish the throne of your kingdom over Israel forever, just as I spoke to your father David, saying "You shall not lack a man on the throne of Israel."

But its hearers would also remember Solomon's failures: his harsh corvée system, his indulging of foreign wives, and the nation's split after his death.

Psalm 72 ends with the words "The prayers of David son of Jesse are ended." David moves almost completely out of the picture. Psalm 72 continues the "Who are we?" portion of the story of the Psalter. Solomon had a magnificent reign, hallmarked by his building of the temple at Jerusalem. But the downward spiral of ancient Israel's political career began even before Solomon's death. Psalm 72 anticipates the overwhelming cry of the lamenting questions in Psalm 89.

(Philadelphia: Fortress Press, 1979) 516.

Chapter 8

Book Three

Psalm 73

Book Three of the Psalter opens with a psalm which Walter Brueggemann maintains is placed at a "faultline" in the Psalter, "that is, the dis-
ruption of faith after the failure of Solomon."[1] Psalm 73 is a Psalm of
Asaph. Fifteen of the seventeen psalms in Book Three are attributed to
Asaph and Qorah.[2] Only one psalm, Psalm 86, is attributed to David.
Recall that all of Book One's psalms are "of David," and in Book Two,
eighteen of the thirty-two psalms are associated with him. With the close
of Psalm 72, David moves to the background. The focus is now on
David's descendants, who will determine the future of ancient Israel.
Psalms of the community, rather than psalms of the individual, are the
predominant type in Book Three.

Asaph is credited with twelve psalms in the Psalter, Psalms 50 and
73–83. The Chronicler states that Asaph is the brother of Heman, the son
of Berechiah, a descendant of Levi through Gershom, and part of one of
the great families or guilds of musicians and singers in preexilic Israel.[3]
Harry P. Nasuti asserts that by the early postexilic era the Asaphites were
the only singers' group in the cultic community.[4] The author of 1 Esdras
writes that one segment of those returning to the land of Israel after the
Exile were "The Levites: . . . The temple singers: the descendants of

---

[1]Walter Brueggemann, "Bounded by Obedience and Praise: The Psalms as
Canon," JSOT 50 (1991): 82-83.

[2]The remaining psalm, Psalm 89, is ascribed to Ethan, who was a temple
singer along with Heman and Asaph. See 1 Chronicles 15:19.

[3]See 1 Chronicles 6:39; 25:1,2; and 2 Chronicles 5:12.

[4]For a complete treatment, see Harry P. Nasuti, *Tradition History and the
Psalms of Asaph*, SBLDS 88 (Atlanta: Scholars Press, 1988).

Asaph, one hundred twenty-eight."[5] The songs in the Psalter which are
attributed to Asaph were probably part of a much larger collection of
songs, of which the twelve we find in the Psalter became "normative and
authoritative" for the postexilic community.[6]

Psalm 73, the opening of Book Three, stands in interesting contrast
to Psalm 42, with which Book Two begins. In Psalm 42, the psalmist is
far away from God. The enemy taunts the psalmist with "Where is your
God?" and the psalmist debates with the self over whether to despair or
to hope. In Psalm 73, the psalmist speaks directly to God and expresses
a strong sense of nearness to God. But the feelings of despair and of
hope are much the same in the two psalms:

> My tears have been food to me day and night,
> . . . O my God, my being is sunk down within me. (42:4, 7; EVV 3, 6)

> For I have been stricken all day long,
>   And chastened every morning. (73:14)

> YHWH will command his *hesed* in the daytime;
>   And His song will be with me in the night. (42:9; EVV 8)

> I am continually with You;
>   You have taken hold of my right hand. (73:23)

In Psalm 73, although the psalmist is near God, all still is not well.

We may divide the psalm into three sections. In verses 1-12, the
psalmist laments the security, well-being, and arrogance of the רשעים
(wicked). The wicked are prospering, growing fat, and mocking God
(vv. 4-10), while the psalmist is on slippery ground:

> . . . almost my feet stumbled;
>   Almost my steps slipped.
> For I was envious of the boasters,
>   The well-being of the רשעים (wicked) I saw. (vv. 2,3)

---

[5] 1 Esdras 5:26-27. See also Ezra 2:4 and Nehemiah 7:44.
[6] 1 Chronicles 16:7-36, which parallels Psalm 105, contains another example
of a Psalm of Asaph.

The psalm begins, however, with "Surely God is good to Israel,"[7] echoing the declaration in Psalm 1 that all will go well for the person who meditates on YHWH's Torah and doesn't associate with the wicked. Psalm 73 reiterates the theological assumptions of Psalm 1 and affirms confidence in the basic tenets of Torah.

Psalm 73 is classified, along with Psalm 1, as a wisdom psalm and is often compared with the Book of Job.[8] In fact, we might subtitle Psalm 73 the "Little Job of the Psalter." The psalmist is envious of those who prosper despite their blatant disregard for God and questions whether conventional theology and mores still hold true in life.

Humankind in the ancient Near East believed in a basic moral governance of the universe. Act and consequence were connected in daily life. Thus, the good prospered and the wicked perished. Sages, wisdom teachers, and writers taught that there was a fundamental order in the world which could be discerned by experience, that the gods had established the order, and all of humankind was bound by the rules governing that order.[9] But Psalm 73, along with other wisdom compositions like Job and Ecclesiastes, addresses the realities of everyday life. Here, the psalmist finds no reasoned connection between righteousness and reward, wickedness and punishment. The wicked prosper and the righteous suffer.

---

[7]I adopt here an unemended reading of the MT's אך טוב לישראל אלהים. While many emend the text to אך טוב לישׁר אל אלהים (see RSV and NRSV, for example.), I am especially persuaded by Walter Brueggemann's argument for leaving the text as it stands. See "Bounded by Praise and Obedience: The Psalms as Canon," 83.

[8]See, e.g., J. Clinton McCann, Jr., *A Theological Introduction to the Book of Psalms* (Nashville: Abingdon Press, 1993) 140-44; James F. Ross, "Psalm 73," in *Israelite Wisdom: Theological and Literary Essays in Honor of Samuel Terrien*, ed. John G. Gammie et al. (Missoula MT: Scholars Press, 1978) 161-75; and Martin Buber, "The Heart Determines: Psalm 73," in *Theodicy in the Old Testament*, ed. James L. Crenshaw (Philadelphia: Fortress Press, 1983) 109-18.

[9]For detailed treatments, see James L. Crenshaw, *Old Testament Wisdom: An Introduction* (Atlanta: John Knox Press, 1981); Joseph Blenkinsopp, *Wisdom and Law in the Old Testament* (Oxford: Oxford University Press, 1983); Roland E. Murphy, *The Tree of Life: An Exploration of Biblical Wisdom Literature* (New York: Doubleday, 1990); and *The Sage in Israel and the Ancient Near East*, ed. John G. Gammie and Leo G. Perdue (Winona Lake IN: Eisenbrauns, 1990).

The ancient Israelites were not the only people to question the conventional wisdom of the ancient Near East. *The Eloquent Peasant* is a story from early second millennium Egypt in which a man is unjustly arrested and imprisoned. The pharaoh is pleased with the rhetoric that the man uses to declare his innocence, and so orders that the man be held just to amuse the pharaoh. The words of the eloquent peasant sound much like our psalmist:

> Goodness is destroyed, none adhere to it,
> To fling falsehood's back to the ground.
> If the ferry is grounded, wherewith does one cross?[10]

I Will Praise the Lord of Wisdom and *The Babylonian Theodicy*, both from late second millennium Mesopotamia, also deal with issues of the wicked prospering and the righteous suffering:

> What is good in one's sight is evil for a god.
> What is bad in one's own kind is good for his god.
> Who can understand the counsel of the gods in the midst of heaven?
> The plan of a god is deep waters, who can comprehend it?[11]

The author of Psalm 73 questions whether righteousness is worthwhile:

> Surely in emptiness I have cleansed my heart,
>   and I have washed my hands in innocence. (v. 13)

Verses 13-17 are the second division of the psalm. The psalmist is tempted to believe that there is no benefit for the one who obeys the instructions of YHWH, that faithfulness is ריק (emptiness). In Psalm 2:1, the nations and the people are "meditating or plotting ריק." In Psalm 73, the psalmist fears that righteousness is ריק. But in verse 15, the psalmist realizes that if one rejects the basic tenets of Torah, then "Behold, I have betrayed the generation of Your children." The psalmist's remembrance of belonging, of being part of an ongoing community, provides the assurance required to maintain identity and direction.

---

[10]Miriam Lichtheim, *Ancient Egyptian Literature*, vol. 1 (Berkeley: University of California Press, 1973) 177.

[11]James B. Pritchard, ed., *Ancient Near Eastern Texts Relating to the Old Testament*, 3rd ed. (Princeton: Princeton University Press, 1969) 435-40 and 601-604.

This sense of community identity is solidified in the act of worship in the מקדשי־אל (v. 17) The psalmist experiences the nearness and presence of God in the "sanctuaries."[12] At the sanctuaries, the psalmist returns to the "sober, simplistic piety" of Psalm 1 and Psalm 73:1.[13] God is near. That is all that matters.

Verses 18-28 form the third and final division of Psalm 73. In these verses, the wicked are set in slippery places (v. 18), and the psalmist is secure because God is continually present (v. 23). The psalm ends:

> For behold, the ones far from You will perish.
>   You have destroyed all who are unfaithful to You.
> But (as for) me,
>   the nearness of God to me is good. (vv. 27-28)

The psalm ends as it begins. God is good (v. 1) and the nearness of God is good (v. 28), despite the well-being of the רשעים. Brueggemann observes:

> No judgment is finally made whether the world is morally coherent or not, whether Psalm 1 is true or not, whether Psalm 73:1 is sustainable or not.[14]

God is present. That is all that matters.

After witnessing the prosperity of the wicked during the destruction of Jerusalem, the exile in Babylon, and during the return to the land, the postexilic community may have been tempted to let their feet stumble and their steps slip (73:2). The psalms of David in Books One and Two evoke a nostalgia for the days of David's kingdom and an independent nation of ancient Israel. But the great number of laments in the first two Books remind the readers/hearers that all was not well even in those days. With the final words of Psalm 72, "the prayers of David . . . are ended" (v. 20), a new chapter in the story of the Psalter begins. The shaping community was not finished defining itself, finding answers to the question, "Who are we?" More of the story remains after the reign of

---

[12]For a full discussion on the translation and meaning of מקדשי־אל, see Ross, "Psalm 73," 165-67.

[13]Brueggemann, "Bounded by Obedience and Praise: The Psalms as Canon," 85.

[14]Ibid., 86.

Solomon, and that story is told in Book Three. Psalm 73 reminds the reader/hearer of the one firm reality in the life of ancient Israel—YHWH is טוב (good).

The postexilic community is assured that despite the despair that tempts them to forget the Torah and YHWH's goodness, YHWH is present, and that is all that they need. David's dynasty in the person of Solomon and his successors failed, but YHWH has not failed. YHWH will provide the stability in a world that is no longer grounded in traditional wisdom. The people must remain a part of the community of YHWH, and then ancient Israel can survive.

"Begin at the beginning." The beginning of the Psalter rehearses the story of ancient Israel for a postexilic audience: the rise of ancient Israel under the leadership of Kings David and Solomon (Books One and Two) and the demise of ancient Israel, the destruction of Jerusalem at the hands of the Babylonians, and the Exile (Book Three). Good times were mixed with bad. Prosperity was mixed with misfortune. But the message is clear. The sole ingredients, the hermeneutical underpinnings, for the survival of ancient Israel are YHWH and YHWH's Torah.[15] These two ingredients allowed ancient Israel to survive through centuries of its historic past. And they will sustain Israel into its postexilic future.

Psalm 89

Book Three of the Psalter ends with an overwhelming cry of lament. Psalm 89 is classified as a royal psalm, but it is very different from the other royal psalms in the Psalter.[16] In Psalm 89, the psalmist pleads with YHWH to be faithful to the covenant with David, but that covenant is

---

[15]See James L. Mays, *The Lord Reigns: A Theological Handbook to the Psalms* (Louisville: Westminster/John Knox Press, 1994) 132.

[16]For full treatments of and comments on Psalm 89, see Marvin E. Tate, *Psalms 51–100*, WBC 20 (Dallas: Word Books, 1990) 406-30; H.-J. Kraus, *Psalms 60–150: A Commentary*, trans. H. C. Oswald (Minneapolis: Augsburg Publishing House, 1988) 197-211; and Gerald H. Wilson, *The Editing of the Hebrew Psalter*, SBLDS 76 (Chico CA: Scholars Press, 1985) 212-14. J. Clinton McCann, Jr. suggests that Psalm 89 anticipates for the reader/hearer two other royal psalms placed near the ends of Books Four and Five, Psalms 101 and 144 (correspondence from J. Clinton McCann, Jr., May 1995).

viewed as part of a distant past.[17] The covenant promises are at an end. Gerald Wilson remarks that

> At the conclusion of the third book . . . the impression left is one of a covenant remembered, but a covenant *failed*. The Davidic covenant introduced in Psalm 2 has come to nothing and the combination of three books concludes with the anguished cry of the Davidic descendants.[18]

Psalm 89 ends with question after question to YHWH: "How long, O YHWH? Will You hide Yourself forever?" (verse 47; EVV 46) "Where are Your former חסדים, O YHWH?" (verse 50; EVV 49).[19] It powerfully outlines the contradiction between old promises and understandings of the ways of God and the actualities of the history of ancient Israel.[20] History has not turned out as the people hoped and expected. And so they are full of questions. Psalm 73 reminded the people not to despair in their present circumstances. But at the end of Book Three, the volume of lament seems to have overpowered the confidence expressed at the beginning of the Book. Psalm 89 ends in lament, without an expression of confidence in YHWH that is normally found in the psalms of lament.[21]

The story of the Psalter is YHWH's instruction to the postexilic community in which the people can find answers to the questions "Who are we?" and "What are we to do?" Books One, Two, and Three answer the question "Who are we?" The ancient Israelites were the chosen people of YHWH who once had a king and all the trappings of nationhood. But those days ended with the destruction of Jerusalem and the exile. The postexilic community was back in its own land. The temple was rebuilt, the cult was restored, but the people had no king and no

---

[17]See Gerald H. Wilson, "The Use of Royal Psalms at the 'Seams' of the Hebrew Psalter," JSOT 35 (1986): 90-91.

[18]Wilson, *The Editing of the Hebrew Psalter*, 213.

[19]In 2 Samuel 7:15 YHWH states, "but my חסד shall not depart from him, as I took it away from Saul." In Psalm 89 the psalmist asks YHWH where are the former חסדים. And in the opening psalm of Book Four, the psalmist asks YHWH to "Return . . . and satisfy us with your חסד (90:12-13).

[20]Tate, *Psalms 51–100*, 428. James L. Mays describes Psalm 89 as a "shattering quandry." Mays, *The Lord Reigns*, 105.

[21]See W. H. Bellinger, Jr., *Psalms: Reading and Studying the Book of Praises* (Peabody MA: Hendrickson Publishers, 1990) 46.

political identity. Book Three ends with questions that move the reader on to the second question of identity.

"What are we to do?" Books Four and Five of the Psalter will remind the people that YHWH was their king long before the days of David and Solomon and will tell them that YHWH continues to be their king, with all the identity and stability that kingship entails. YHWH is near. YHWH and the Torah are all that matter. But how will these "facts" shape and assure the survival of the postexilic community? "Begin at the beginning. . . . Go on until you come to the end."[22] We turn now to Books Four and Five of the Psalter. That which slumbers is almost roused.[23]

---

[22]Lewis Carroll, *Alice in Wonderland*, 2nd ed., A Norton Critical Edition, ed. Donald J. Gray (New York: W. W. Norton, 1992) 94.

[23]William G. Braude, *The Midrash on Psalms*, vol. 1 (New Haven CT: Yale University Press, 1959) 50.

Chapter 9

Book Four

Introduction

"Go on till you come to the end: then stop."[1]

Psalms 1, 2, and 3 begin the beginning of the Psalter; Psalm 90 begins the end. It opens Book Four, at the heart of which are located the so-called יהוה מלך psalms, Psalms 93 and 95 through 99. Psalm 90 is a turning point in the Psalter; it focuses the reader/hearer's attention in a new direction.[2] What is the significance and role of Psalm 90 in the shape of the Psalter? We will begin by examining the larger context of the psalm.

Books One, Two, and Three of the Psalter focus on the reigns of David and David's descendants. The "story" of the three books is delineated as early as Psalm 3. Ancient Israel had once been an independent nation under the leadership of David. But dark days descended, and Babylon destroyed Jerusalem and carried the people away into exile. At the end of Book Three comes Psalm 89's anguished lament over the failure of the Davidic covenant. The psalmist pleads with YHWH to remember the covenant with David and the חסד with which YHWH dealt with Israel in the past.

---

[1]Lewis Carroll, *Alice in Wonderland*, 2nd. ed., A Norton Critical Edition, ed. Donald J. Gray (New York: Norton, 1992) 94.

[2]See Gerald Wilson, *The Editing of the Hebrew Psalter*, SBLDS 76 (Chico CA: Scholars Press, 1985) 214-19; Walter Brueggemann, *The Message of the Psalms: A Theological Commentary* (Minneapolis: Augsburg Publishing House, 1984) 110-15; Gerhard von Rad, *God at Work in Israel*, trans. John H. Marks (Nashville: Abingdon Press, 1980) 210-23; and J. Clinton McCann, Jr., *A Theological Introduction to the Book of Psalms: The Psalms as Torah* (Nashville: Abingdon Press, 1993) 155-62.

How long, O YHWH?
    Will You hide Yourself forever?
Will Your wrath burn like fire?
    . . . Where are Your former חסדים, O YHWH,
    Which You swore to David in Your faithfulness?
                                        (vv. 47, 50; EVV 46, 49)

But the psalm ends with no answer from YHWH, and Book Three closes with the usual benediction, "Blessed be YHWH forever. Amen and Amen."

David's dynasty failed, but the reader/hearer will find that YHWH has not failed. YHWH will provide the stability in a world that is no longer grounded in established modes of stability. Books One, Two, and Three of the Psalter answer for the postexilic Israelite community the question "Who are we?" They were a people who once had a king of YHWH's choosing and a nation which stretched "from Dan to Beersheba." But those days ended with the destruction of Jerusalem and the exile.

The people were now back in their own land. Their temple was rebuilt, but they had no king, no court, no political identity within the ancient Near Eastern cultural structure. After Books One, Two, and Three rehearse for the people their history—the answer to the question "Who are we?"—Books Four and Five give an answer to the question "What are we to do?" They remind the postexilic community that YHWH was their king long before the days of David and Solomon and tell the people that YHWH will continue to be their king with all the identity and stability that kingship entails. Ancient Israel can survive if it relies completely on the two tenets by which Israel survived through centuries of its historical past—YHWH's תורה (Psalm 1) and YHWH's kingship (Psalm 2).

Psalm 90

How does Psalm 90 in its canonical position function as the turning point in the Psalter? Psalm 90 is the only psalm in the Psalter which is ascribed to Moses. The superscription reads, "A prayer of Moses, the man of God." Within the story of the Psalter, such an ascription is fitting. The focus of the Psalter up to this point has been the kingship of David and David's descendants and on the failure of that kingship.[3] Moses rep-

---

[3]Remember that in Books One, Two, and Three of the Psalter, fifty-six of the psalms are ascribed to David, while another twenty-four are ascribed to members

resents a different time in the history of ancient Israel, a time before the Davidic covenant, before the monarchy, before the judges, before the settlement in Palestine.

The Deuteronomistic History tells us that YHWH made a covenant with ancient Israel long before the time of David, during the time of the wilderness wanderings.[4] The prophet Hosea views this time as the "honeymoon" period of ancient Israel's history. He writes:

Therefore, behold, I will allure Israel,
    bring her into the wilderness and speak kindly to her.
Then I will give her her vineyards from there,
    and the Valley of Achor as a door of hope.
And she will sing there as in the days of her youth,
    as in the day when she came up from the land of Egypt.
                                        (Hosea 2:14-15)

The ancient Israelites had to rely completely on YHWH to provide for, sustain, and protect them during the wilderness wanderings. YHWH was the sole source of their survival. In Exodus 15 and Deuteronomy, Moses sings songs to YHWH and describes YHWH in very kingly language.

I will sing to YHWH for in triumph He has triumphed,
The horse and its rider he has thrown into the sea.
. . . YHWH is a man of war, YHWH is his name.
. . . YHWH will rule (ימלך) forever and ever. (Exodus 15:1, 3, 8)

For I proclaim the name of YHWH;
    Ascribe greatness to our God.
The rock. His work is perfect,
    For all His ways are just;
A God of faithfulness and without injustice,
    Righteous and upright is He. (Deuteronomy 32:3, 4)

In Deuteronomy 33:5, Moses declares that YHWH is king over Israel with the words ויהי בישרון מלך.[5]

---

of David's and Solomon's royal courts. In Books Four and Five, however, only fifteen psalms are attributed to David.

[4]See Exodus 20.

[5]For a full discussion of the linguistic links between Exodus 15, Deuteronomy 32:1–33:29, and Psalm 90, see Marvin E. Tate, *Psalms 51–100*, WBC 20 (Dallas: Word Books, 1990) 438.

After the ancient Israelites settled in the land of Canaan, however, they demanded that Samuel anoint a human king for them:

> Now appoint a king [מלך] for us to judge us like all the nations.
>
> (1 Samuel 8:5)

Samuel was displeased, but YHWH said to him:

> Listen to the voice of the people in regard to all that they say to you, for they have not rejected you, but they have rejected Me from being king (ממלך) over them. (1 Samuel 8:7)

So Samuel anointed Saul as king over Israel, and from that time until the exile, the people had an earthly king "to judge them," just as the other peoples in the ancient Near East. YHWH even made a covenant with David that David's throne would be established forever. But a Davidic king had not always been a part of ancient Israel's history. The superscription of Psalm 90 reminded the postexilic community that before David was king over them, YHWH was king.

Did the author of Psalm 90 give the psalm the title "A prayer of Moses, the man of God"? Or was the superscription added to the psalm after it was already part of the authoritative literature of the cultic community? Psalm 90 certainly has strong linguistic ties to other stories about Moses in the Hebrew scriptures. The postexilic reader/hearer would recall that Deuteronomy 33 is the only place in the Hebrew Bible other than Psalm 90 where Moses is called "the man of God" (איש אלהים). In that passage, Moses blesses Israel on the plains of Moab before his death and before the people enter the "promised" land. The words of Moses in Deuteronomy 33 come at a crucial juncture in the life of ancient Israel. Israel is poised on the edge of Canaan, ready to enter the land YHWH had promised them. Psalm 90 represents another critical juncture in ancient Israel's life. In the story of the Psalter, Israel is in exile and waiting to return to the land that YHWH had promised them. And again, "Moses, the man of God" speaks.

Psalm 90:2 describes the creation work of YHWH with the verbs ילד and חיל. Deuteronomy 32:18 uses the same verbs to describe the work of YHWH:

> You neglected the Rock who begot (ילד) you,
> And forgot the god who gave you birth (חיל).

In Deuteronomy 32:36, Moses tells the ancient Israelites that YHWH "will have compassion (נחם) upon His servants (עבדים)." In Psalm 90:13, the psalmist entreats YHWH to "have compassion (נחם) on Your servants (עבדים)."

Finally, Psalm 90 contains two unusual plural forms, ימות and שׁנות, which are found in only one other place in the Hebrew Bible, Deuteronomy 32:7.[6]

The strongest tie between Moses and Psalm 90 is found in Exodus 32. Only in Exodus 32 and Psalm 90 does a human being admonish God to "turn" (שׁוב) and repent (נחם). And in both passages, Moses is the human being who commands YHWH not to act against the ancient Israelites in retribution for their sins.

> Return (שׁובה) O YHWH; How long will it be?
> And repent (הנחם) because of your servants. (Psalm 90:13)

> Turn (שׁוב) from the heat of your anger and repent (הנחם).
> (Exodus 32:12b)

David Noel Freedman writes:

> Whoever put the heading on Psalm 90, attributing it to "Moses, the man of God," must have known that Moses alone tells God to "turn" and "repent." Another possibility—and a more likely one in my view [and in this writer's view]—is that the composer of the psalm based it on the episode in Exodus 32 and imagined in poetic form how Moses may have spoken in the circumstances of Exodus 32.[7]

The Targum to Psalm 90, in fact, titles it "A prayer of Moses the prophet, when the people of Israel sinned in the desert." For a second time in the history of ancient Israel, Moses will attempt to dissuade YHWH from destroying the chosen people.

Not just Psalm 90, but the whole fourth book of the Psalter, is dominated by the person of Moses. Outside of Book Four, Moses is mentioned only once in the Psalter (77:21). In Book Four, he is referred to seven times (90:1; 99:6; 103:7; 105:26; 106:16, 23, 32).[8] The title of

---

[6]See Tate, *Psalms 51–100*, 438.

[7]See David Noel Freedman, "Other than Moses . . . Who Asks (or Tells) God to Repent?" *Bible Review* 1/4 (1985): 59.

[8]Marvin Tate, in fact, describes Book Four as a "Moses Book." See *Psalms*

Psalm 90, in its canonical position, cues the reader/hearer to the shaping community's understanding of Psalm 90. The psalm sends the reader/hearer back to the beginning of ancient Israel's history, before the time of the monarchy, when Israel relied completely on YHWH for sustenance and protection. And that is a key role of Psalm 90 in the story of the Psalter. But Psalm 90 also performs the literary role of sending the reader/hearer back to the beginning of the Psalter, back to Psalms 1 and 2 and the ideas of YHWH's Torah and YHWH's kingship.

Psalms 1 and 2 introduce the idea of kingship in the story of the Psalter. Psalm 90 takes up where they leave off. After an interval of Davidic kingship which has failed (Psalms 3–89), Psalm 90 draws the reader/hearer's attention right back to the beginning, back to Psalms 1 and 2 and the idea of YHWH as king. The pressing need of the postexilic community was identity and stability. Kingship—for ancient Israel, a king of the Davidic line—was the remembered pattern for identity and stability. But postexilic Israel could not have a human king. The means for achieving survival and maintaining identity was to acknowledge YHWH as king (Psalm 2:11) and to obey YHWH's instruction in the תורה (Psalm 1:2).

Verses 7-9 of Psalm 90 echo thoughts the reader/hearer encountered in Psalms 1 and 2. In verse 7, we read:

> For we have been consumed by your anger (אף),
> and by your wrath (חמה) we have been terrified (בהל).

which echoes Psalm 2:5's "Then he will speak to them in his anger (אף) and terrify (בהל) them in his fury." Most interesting is verse 9's

> For all our days have declined in your fury;
> we have finished our years like a musing (הגה).

These words echo for the Hebrew reader/hearer the words of Psalm 1:2, "But his delight is in the torah of YHWH and in his torah he meditates (יהגה) day and night," and the words of Psalm 2:1, "Why are the nations conspiring and the peoples plotting empty things" (יהגו, also from the root הגה). The Hebrew word הגה is interesting in its contexts in Psalms 1, 2, and 90. Psalm 1 encourages its readers/hearers to meditate (הגה, v. 2) on the instruction of YHWH in order to find true wisdom and

---

51–100, xxvi.

understanding. In Psalm 2, the nations are meditating (הגה, v. 2), but in order to conspire together against YHWH and against YHWH's anointed. This type of meditating kindles YHWH's anger (אף, v. 5) and fury, and thus YHWH will terrify (בהל, v. 5) them. In Psalm 90, not the nations, but the Israelites themselves have kindled YHWH's anger (אף, v. 7) and wrath (המה, v. 7), and YHWH has terrified (בהל, v. 7) them. And so the years of ancient Israel's history have been useless meditating (הגה, v. 9).

הגה is used only twenty-two times in the entire Hebrew Bible, and only ten times in the Psalter. Its meaning ranges from murmur, mutter, growl, sigh, or moan to meditate or muse.[9] Translations of the Psalter render הגה differently in its occurrences in Psalms 1, 2, and 90. In the KJV, the word is translated "meditate" in Psalm 1, "imagine" in Psalm 2, and "a tale" in Psalm 90. In the RSV, it is "meditate" in Psalm 1, "plot" in Psalm 2, and "a sigh" in Psalm 90. The NASV translates the word as "meditate," "devise," and "a sigh or whisper" in the three psalms, while the NIV renders it as "meditate," "plot," and "a moan." The impact of the repetition of this word has been lost in translation, but the ancient Israelite reader/hearer must have been struck by the use of this uncommon word in Psalms 1, 2, and 90. Ancient Israel's attempt at "self-rule" in the Davidic dynasty is as empty as the plotting of YHWH's enemies in Psalm 2. Psalm 89 confirms the collapse of the house of David; Psalm 90 redirects the attention of the reader/hearer back to the beginning.

What must Israel do? Psalm 2 has already given the answer. In Psalm 2, YHWH is enthroned in heaven, looking down upon the scene on earth (v. 4). For a time, there was a king of YHWH's choosing in Zion. But that time has ended. Psalm 2:11 and 12 read:

> Serve YHWH with fear;
>   with trembling kiss his feet.
> Lest he become angry
>   and you perish in the way.[10]

Psalm 90 tells the ancient Israelites that they must now go back to the beginning—back to the days before David, before the judges, before the settlement of the land. YHWH must be their king; but YHWH is angry

---

[9]A. Negoiṭă, הָגָה hāghāh, in *Theological Dictionary of the Old Testament*, vol. 3 (Grand Rapids MI: Eerdmans, 1978) 321.

[10]See p. 47.

with ancient Israel just as YHWH was angry with them in the wilderness. Moses changed YHWH's mind in the wilderness. Moses can change YHWH's mind now. Psalm 90 recalls Moses's plea to YHWH in Exodus 32 not to destroy the people. In Exodus 32, Moses is successful; YHWH relents and spares ancient Israel.

Can Moses's plea to YHWH be successful a second time and in a new place in ancient Israel's history? Apparently it can. The remainder of Book Four of the Psalter is a celebration of the kingship of YHWH. David Howard analyzes the structure of Book Four as concentric pattern with psalms about Moses (Psalms 90 and 106) at the edges and the "classic kingship of YHWH psalms" in the center.[11] Ancient Israel will survive the uncertainties of vassal existence. McCann observes that

> Book Four affirms that God reigns, suggesting that the Davidic monarchy is not indispensable. In short, God is the only necessity for the life of God's people. Such has been the case—"in all generations."[12]

Thus we may say that the shapers of the Psalter placed Psalm 90 at the beginning of Book Four to mark a turning point in the Psalter. It sends the reader/hearer back to the beginning of ancient Israel's relationship with YHWH *and* back to the beginning of the Psalter. Psalm 90 is an updated intercession of Moses for a new generation of ancient Israelites and a turning point in the Psalter.[13] The empty meditating (הגה) is replaced with a new confidence in the reign of YHWH.

Psalm 106

Book Four ends with Psalm 106, an interesting psalm in its context in the Psalter. It begins and ends with הללו יה, and it is a rehearsal of historical events in the life of ancient Israel. These two characteristics by no means make Psalm 106 unique. In Book Four, Psalms 104, 105, and

---

[11]David M. Howard, "A Contextual Reading of Psalms 90–94," in *The Shape and Shaping of the Psalter*, ed. J. Clinton McCann, Jr., JSOTSup 159 (Sheffield UK: Sheffield Academic Press, 1993) 109.

[12]McCann, *A Theological Introduction to the Book of Psalms*, 156.

[13]McCann and Beth Tanner speculate that Psalm 90 represents how the composer of the psalm, or the shapers of the Psalter, imagined in poetic form how Moses may have spoken to the "monumental crisis posed by the loss of land, temple, and monarchy." McCann and Tanner, "Moses, Psalm 90, and the Shape of the Psalter," unpub. paper, SBL Books of Psalms Group (1992) 4.

106 contain the phrase יה הללו. Psalms 104 and 105 close with the phrase. But Psalm 106 both opens and closes with it (vv. 1 and 48).[14]

Other psalms in the Psalter also outline the great historical events in the life of ancient Israel. Psalms 105 and 136, for instance, recall YHWH's covenant with Abraham (105:9), YHWH's protection of Joseph (105:17-22), the escape from Egypt (105:26-41), the wilderness wanderings (136:16), and the safe entrance into the promised land (136:21). But Psalm 106 emphasizes some less positive events in the life of ancient Israel. Beginning in verse 6, the psalm reminds the reader/hearer that Israel's ancestors did not understand YHWH's works in Egypt (v. 7), rebelled at the Reed Sea (v. 7), put YHWH to the test in the wilderness (v. 14), envied Moses and Aaron (v. 16), made a golden calf at Horeb (v. 19), despised the promised land (v. 24), worshipped other gods (v. 28), and did not drive out the foreign peoples from their land (v. 34).

Psalms 105 and 136 emphasize YHWH's great redeeming acts in the life of ancient Israel. Psalm 106 emphasizes the rebellious response of Israel to YHWH's acts.[15] And once again, the reader/hearer is reminded that Moses persuaded YHWH not to destroy the people:

Moses, His chosen one stood in the breach before Him,
To turn away His wrath (חמה) from destroying them. (v. 23)

Psalm 106 has been classified as both a community hymn and a community lament.[16] Is Psalm 106 hymn or lament? Is there something

---

[14]Some scholars maintain that the הללו יה with which Psalm 104 closes should actually be placed at the beginning of Psalm 105, so that both 105 and 106 open and close with the phrase. The Septuagint places the הללו יה of Psalm 104 at the beginning of Psalm 105. For a full discussion, see Bruce K. Waltke, "Superscripts, Postscripts, or Both," JBL 110 (1991): 583-96.

[15]See James L. Mays, *The Lord Reigns: A Theological Handbook to the Psalms* (Louisville: Westminster/John Knox Press, 1994) 133.

[16]Hermann Gunkel and Claus Westermann classify the psalm as a communal complaint. Gunkel, *Die Psalmen* (Göttingen: Vandenhoeck & Ruprecht, 1929) 464-65, and Westermann, *Praise and Lament in the Psalms*, trans. K. R. Crim and R. N. Soulen (Atlanta: John Knox Press, 1981) 141. Leslie C. Allen writes that Psalm 106 is "a community complaint strongly marked by hymnic features." Allen, *Psalms 101–150*, WBC 21 (Waco TX: Word Books, 1983) 50. H.-J. Kraus calls it a hymn of a "grand historical narrative." But he recognizes the lament elements within its structure. "The more the disclosure of the guilt of Israel emerges . . . beside the thankful praise of Yahweh's wonders and proofs of good-

about the canonical position of Psalm 106 and its role in the story of the Psalter that provides clues about its shape and purpose?

Books One, Two, and Three of the Psalter tell the story of the failure of the monarchy in ancient Israel. The covenant YHWH made with David is at an end. Book Four opens with "A Psalm of Moses, the man of God," a psalm which pushes the reader/hearer back to the time before the ancient Israelites had a king, before they had judges, before they settled in the land of Israel, back to the time when YHWH was the sole sustainer of the people. In the middle of Book Four, the יהוה מלך psalms celebrate the kingship of YHWH over all the earth.

The community that shaped the Psalter is delineating in Books Four and Five an answer to the question, "What are we to do in our present situation?" The answer is to go back to the time before YHWH's covenant with David, back to the time when Israel relied solely on YHWH. Let YHWH be king once again.

> YHWH reigns, He is clothed with majesty;
>   YHWH has clothed and girded Himself with strength;
> Indeed, the world is firmly established,
>   it will not be moved.
> Thy throne is established from of old;
>   Thou art from everlasting. (Psalm 93:1, 2)

At the end of Book Four are Psalms 105 and 106. Psalm 105 is a hymn celebrating the marvelous deeds of YHWH on behalf of ancient Israel. Psalm 106 also outlines the marvelous deeds of YHWH on behalf of ancient Israel.[17] But Psalm 106 concentrates on ancient Israel's failure to trust YHWH, despite YHWH's saving acts. The message to the postexilic community is clear. "Go back to the time when Israel relied solely on YHWH. But remember that even in the days of your ancestors, in the time of your escape from Egypt, during the wilderness wanderings, and when you settled in the land of Israel, all was not well." The ancient Israelites

---

ness, the more the prayer of repentance and petition asserts itself in the frame-work." H.-J. Kraus, *Psalms 60–150: A Commentary*, trans. H. C. Oswald (Minneapolis: Augsburg Publishing House, 1988) 316.

[17]Interestingly, neither psalm mentions David or YHWH's covenant with David. In contrast, Psalm 89 laments the end of David's covenant and pleads with YHWH to remember and restore the Davidic kingship.

had been consistently disobedient and unfaithful to YHWH throughout their history. Despite the fact that YHWH can provide a means for survival in the postexilic world, the people themselves must determine to be faithful to YHWH.

Psalm 106, at the end of Book Four of the Psalter, ends very differently from Psalm 89, at the end of Book Three. Psalm 89 ends with question after question about why ancient Israel is suffering in its present situation. Psalm 106, however, ends, not with questions, but with a simple petition to YHWH:

> Save us, O YHWH our God,
>> And gather us from among the nations,
> To give thanks to Your holy name,
>> And boast in Your praise. (v. 47)

The community which shaped the Psalter placed Psalm 106 at the end of Book Four, which celebrates the kingship of YHWH, to remind the people that YHWH had done marvelous things for Israel in the past. But they had been disobedient and unfaithful in the past, despite YHWH's goodness. In the present situation, YHWH is good to Israel once again, guaranteeing the identity and survival of the postexilic community. Psalm 106 *is* a celebratory hymn, but it is also a lament, a reminder to the people of their disobedience and a warning not to repeat the mistakes of the past.

Chapter 10

Book Five

Psalm 107

Book Five opens with Psalm 107, unquestionably placed at its beginning in answer to the request of the people at the end of Book Four. Psalm 107 begins:

> O give thanks to YHWH, for He is good;
> For his חסד is everlasting.
> Let the redeemed of YHWH say,
> Whom He has redeemed from the hand of the adversary,
> And gathered from the lands,
> From the east and from the west,
> From the north and from the south. (107:1-3)

Four groups of people appear in the liturgy of Psalm 107, who together represent the "redeemed of YHWH" (גאולי יהוה) mentioned in verse 2. Verses 4-9 tell of a group of wanderers, lost in the desert, who finally arrive at their destination. Verses 10-16 tell the story of prisoners who are set free. Verses 17-22 tell of sick persons who are healed. And verses 23-32 are about a group of sailors who are saved from shipwreck.[1]

Each vignette follows a form: (1) a description of the distress (vv. 4-5, 10-12, 17-18, and 23-27); (2) a prayer to YHWH (vv. 6, 13, 19, and 28); (3) details of the deliverance (vv. 7, 14, 20, and 29); and (4) an

---

[1]The "inverted nuns" at verses 21-26 and verse 40 are explained in *Gesenius' Hebrew Grammar*, ed. Emil Kautzsch, trans. A. E. Cowley (Oxford: Clarendon Press, 1910) 5n and 17e, as "a sort of bracket [Hebrew מנזרות—"separated"] to indicate that the verses are out of place" (5n).

expression of thanks (vv. 8-9, 15-16, 21-22, and 30-32).[2] In each of the
four sections, the prayer to YHWH repeats certain words:

Then they cried out (זעק) to YHWH in their trouble (צר);
He delivered/saved them out of their distresses (ממצוקות).
                                                    (107:6, 13, 19, 28)

Are the four vignettes actual accounts of deliverance by YHWH sung
in celebration at a festival? Or is the psalm purely a literary composition,
with the four groups representing, in the words of James L. Mays, "all
those who have experienced the redemption of YHWH"?[3] Whatever the
original *Sitz im Leben* of Psalm 107, its placement in the Psalter by the
shaping community renders it as a hymn celebrating deliverance. And in
the story of the Psalter, that deliverance is from the exile in Babylon. The
shaping community placed the untitled Psalm 107 at the beginning of
Book Five of the Psalter to provide a transition from Book Four (and
Psalm 106) to Book Five.[4]

The original psalm most likely consisted of verses 1-32 and was a
liturgy of thanksgiving used at the preexilic temple. Verses 33-43 were
a separate traditional psalm which the postexilic shaping community
added to Psalm 107's celebration of the goodness of YHWH in order to
remind the reader/hearer that YHWH is not only good, but YHWH is
sovereign as king over all the earth. And YHWH can fulfill the duties of
an earthly king.

The role of the king in the ancient Near East was to guarantee peace,
justice, and right worship.[5] In Psalm 107:33-43, YHWH reigns so that the
hungry and needy can dwell safely in the land, establish a city, sow

---

[2]A. A. Anderson, *The Book of Psalms (73–150)*, NCB (Grand Rapids MI:
Eerdmans, 1972) 749. The final section of the psalm, verses 33-43, is, according
to Kraus, a secondary expansion of the liturgy. He dates the composition of the
final form of the psalm to the postexilic period, but maintains that it "points back
to an older (cultic) perspective of transmission." H.-J. Kraus, *Psalms 60–150: A
Commentary*, trans. H. C. Oswald (Minneapolis: Augsburg, 1989) 327.

[3]James L. Mays, *Psalms*, Interpretation (Louisville: Westminster/John Knox
Press, 1994) 345.

[4]See ibid., 73-81, 214-15.

[5]Keith W. Whitelam, "Israelite Kingship. The Royal Ideology and Its
Opponents," in *The World of Ancient Israel*, ed. R. E. Clements (Cambridge:
Cambridge University Press, 1989) 128.

fields, plant vineyards, and gather a harvest. YHWH pours out contempt
on rulers who oppress the people. The future of the upright is secured
and the unrighteous are left speechless. YHWH as king will provide the
postexilic community with all the identity and security they need to
survive in their new circumstances. Psalm 107:43 asks,

> Who is wise [חכם]? Let him give heed to these things.
> And consider the חסד of YHWH.

I suggested above that verses 33-43 were a separate psalm added to
107:1-32 during the postexilic period by the shapers of the Psalter. The
"wisdom" element of 107:43 carries on throughout Book Five, so that
Book Five seems to bear clearly the stamp of "wisdom" shaping.

Half of all the canonical psalms classified as "wisdom psalms" are
found in Book Five of the Psalter.[6] And many scholars maintain that in
the postexilic period, "wisdom" as a hermeneutical key to understanding
life and the events in life was a prevalent phenomenon.[7] Much of the wisdom material in the Hebrew scriptures achieved its final shape in the postexilic period, including the canonical books of Proverbs and Ecclesiastes.
Psalm 1, as the introduction to the Psalter, certainly prescribes a
"wisdom" approach to reading the Psalter. And the words of Psalm
107:43 suggest that wisdom may be measured by one's heeding of the
חסד of YHWH.

Anthony Ceresko writes that one role of the wisdom movement was
the "ideological function of 'world building'."[8] Walter Brueggemann contends that the wisdom movement engaged in an imaginative process of
"world making." He suggests that

> We do not simply respond to a world that is here, but we engage in con-
> stituting that world by our participation, our actions, and our speech.

---

[6]Psalms 112, 119, 127, 128, and 133.

[7]See, e.g., Anthony R. Ceresko, "The Sage in the Psalms," in *The Sage in
Israel and the Ancient Near East*, ed. John G. Gammie and Leo G. Perdue
(Winona Lake IN: Eisenbrauns, 1990) 217-30; Joseph Blenkinsopp, *Wisdom and
Law in the Old Testament* (Oxford: Oxford University Press, 1983); and James
L. Crenshaw, *Old Testament Wisdom: An Introduction* (Atlanta: John Knox
Press, 1981), 11-65. Psalm 1, as an introduction to the Psalter, certainly
prescribes a "wisdom" approach to reading the Psalter.

[8]Ceresko, "The Sage in the Psalms," 218.

> The human agent, then, is a constitutive part of the enterprise, which
> means that the shape of reality in part awaits our shaping adherence.[9]

The story of the Psalter reflects the postexilic Israelite community's shaping of identity—their world making and world building. The wisdom
movement seems a likely social location for the final shaping of the
Psalter.

Are we then justified in placing the shaping of the Psalter in the
hands of the wisdom movement in postexilic ancient Israel? Yes, if we
remember that the formation of canon, the formation of traditional and
authoritative literature, takes place in community, not in the private
chamber of the scribe or sage. Communities must find value in texts or
those texts will not be preserved. Texts must give life to the communities
that read them and seek answers in them to their existential needs. Thus
they become normative and authoritative.[10] James Sanders reminds us that

> in crisis situations only the old, tried and true has any real authority. A
> new story will not do; only a story with old, recognizable elements has
> the power for life required. . . .[11]

Granted, some "group" of scribes was responsible for the physical copying and passing on of the literature, but the act of shaping canon is a
community process and the text must be studied as the product of
community.

At the same time, a community shaping does not exclude a wisdom
influence. As the postexilic community struggled with the questions
"Who are we?"—stability—and "What are we to do?"—adaptability—the
influence of the wisdom movement seems a natural consequence.[12] In
fact, two of the six wisdom psalms in the Psalter located outside Book

---

[9]Walter Brueggemann, *Israel's Praise: Doxology Against Idolatry and Ideology* (Philadelphia: Fortress Press, 1988) 12-13.

[10]See my discussion in chap. 3.

[11]James A. Sanders, "Adaptable for Life: The Nature and Function of
Canon," in *From Sacred Story to Sacred Text* (Philadelphia: Fortress Press, 1987)
18.

[12]Ceresko writes: "The wisdom school and the psalmist [in this study, the
shaping community] intersect in their common enterprise of maintaining and/or
reshaping this world inhabited by the community of Israel." Ceresko, "The Sage
in the Psalms," 219.

Five occur at key shaping junctures in the Psalter. Psalm 1 is part of the introduction to the story of the Psalter. Psalm 73 opens Book Three.[13]

Psalm 1 at the beginning of Book One reminds the reader/hearer that wisdom lies in the תורה of YHWH and Psalm 107 at the beginning of Book Five acknowledges YHWH as sovereign and able to protect and provide for the postexilic community. Thus wisdom elements begin the beginning and begin the ending of the Psalter. But who is the wise one of Psalm 107:43, the one who is to heed "these things?" The answer to that question may provide a key to another puzzling question of Book Five.

Book Five contains fifteen psalms ascribed to David, the greatest number of psalms of David we have encountered since Book Two.[14] Three psalms of David come immediately after Psalm 107 and eight come at the end of Book Five, just before Psalms 146–150, the group of הללו־יה psalms which conclude the Psalter.

If the Davidic dynasty is at an end and the postexilic community must acknowledge YHWH as their king, then why would so many Davidic psalms occur at this point in the Psalter? By placing fifteen psalms of David in Book Five and, specifically, Psalms 108, 109, and 110 directly after Psalm 107, the shapers of the Psalter suggest that the answer to the question, "Who is the wise one?" of Psalm 107:43 is David, the ideal king of ancient Israel. In Psalm 108:13-14 (EVV 12-13), David sings to YHWH:

Oh give us help against the adversary,
    For deliverance of humankind is in vain.
Through God we shall do valiantly;
    And it is He who will tread down our adversaries.

David gives fealty to YHWH; David acknowledges YHWH as king. The postexilic community will follow.

---

[13]Gerald Wilson maintains that the wisdom element has had the "last word" in the shaping of the Psalter. See "Shaping the Psalter: A Consideration of Editorial Linkage in the Book of Psalms," in *The Shape and Shaping of the Psalter*, ed. J. Clinton McCann, Jr. (Sheffield UK: Sheffield Academic Press, 1993) 80-82.

[14]In Book One, thirty-nine of the forty-one psalms are connected with David; in Book Two, eighteen are connected; in Book Three, only one; and in Book Four, two.

But the strong emphasis on David in the last book of the Psalter performs another function. YHWH is king for now, in the present political
and social circumstances. But the postexilic community retained their
hope for a return to full nationhood. The words of YHWH's covenant with
David still rang strong in the ears of the ancient Israelites:

> YHWH will make a house for you. When your days are complete and
> you lie down with your ancestors, I will raise up your descendant after
> you, who will come forth from you, and I will build a house for my
> name, and I will establish the throne of his kingdom forever. I will be
> a father to him and he will be a son to me. (2 Samuel 7:11-14)

YHWH *had* promised that the throne of David would never be empty. But
in the present circumstances, YHWH will be king, just as YHWH was king
before David's time.

Psalm 145, which comes at the end of Book Five, just before the five
closing הללו־יה psalms, 146–150, is also a psalm of David. In it, the
psalmist, through the voice of David, issues a call to Israel and to all creation to remember, to praise God, and to pass along that memory. David
sings to "my God, the king":

> I will exalt you, my God the king [המלך] . . .
> They will tell of the glory of your kingdom [מלכות]
>   And speak of your might,
> So that all humankind may know of your mighty acts
>   And the glorious splendor of your kingdom.
> Your kingdom is an everlasting kingdom,
>   And your dominion [ממשלה] endures through all generations.
>   (145:1, 11-13)

David, who is no longer king over ancient Israel, David, who has no
hope of any of his heirs ever again being king over ancient Israel, David
acknowledges God as king and sovereign.[15] If David, to whom any hope
of fulfillment of the promises he was given by God seems forever lost,

---

[15]J. Clinton McCann, Jr., in "The Book of Psalms," *New Interpreter's Bible*
4 (Nashville: Abingdon Press, 1996) 690, maintains that in the postexilic period,
the ideology of kingship was transferred from the Davidic dynasty to the whole
people, rather than to YHWH. I don't regard McCann's view in opposition to my
own, but rather as complementary. YHWH is king, and the faithful themselves are
empowered by this fact.

if David can remember and praise God and pass that memory along, then all Israel can and must do the same.

In addition, Psalm 145 is an acrostic poem, a literary device used by wisdom writers. The acrostic form signals the reader/hearer that the psalmist has summed up the memory and praise of YHWH as sovereign from א to ת, and the wisdom format suggests tht the חכם, the "wise one" of Psalm 107 is, indeed, David.[16] David, then, announces and leads the praise of YHWH that takes place in the last five psalms of the Psalter.[17]

> The praise of YHWH my mouth will speak,
> And all flesh will bless his holy name,
> Forever and ever. (145:21)

Psalms 146 through 150

Psalms 146–150 are categorized as general hymns of praise; each begins and ends with הללו־יה; and the final form of each is dated to the postexilic period.[18] But, as is the case with other groups of psalms in the Psalter, Psalms 146–150 is not a haphazard or miscellaneous collection of הלל psalms. It possesses a progression of thought that moves the reader/hearer from the praise of a specific aspect of YHWH's "gracious acts" to a general "unqualified, unencumbered praise."[19]

---

[16]See Leslie C. Allen, *Psalms 101–150*, WBC 21 (Waco TX: Word Books, 1983) 294; James L. Mays, *Psalms*, Interpretation: A Commentary for Teaching and Preaching (Louisville: Westminster/John Knox Press, 1994) 437-38; and John S. Kselman, "Psalm 146 in Its Context," CBQ 50 (1988): 596. Kraus, *Psalms 60–150*, 546, calls it an "alphabetic song."

[17]Frank-Lothar Hossfeld and Erich Zenger, *Die Psalmen I, Psalm 1–50*, NEchtB (Würzburg: Echter Verlag, 1993) 11.

[18]Hermann Gunkel and Joachim Begrich, *Einleitung in die Psalmen* (Göttingen: Vandenhoeck & Ruprecht, 1933) 38; Allen, *Psalms 101–150*, 300-23; Kraus, *Psalms 60–150: A Commentary*, 550-70; and W. H. Bellinger, Jr., *Psalms: Reading and Studying the Book of Praises* (Peabody MA: Hendrickson Publishers, 1990) 81.

[19]Walter Brueggemann, "Bounded by Obedience and Praise: The Psalms as Canon," JSOT 50 (1991): 90.

Psalm 146 is the praise of a single person—most likely David[20]—who knows that YHWH, the God of Jacob, is the ideal king who performs all the requisite kingly duties. The psalmist announces that:

> He upholds the cause of the oppressed
> > and gives food to the hungry.
> YHWH sets prisoners free.
> > YHWH gives sight to the blind.
> YHWH lifts up those who are bowed down;
> > YHWH loves the righteous;
> YHWH protects the strangers;
> > He supports the fatherless and the widow;
> > But He thwarts the way of the wicked.
> YHWH will reign [יִמְלֹךְ] forever. (146:7-10)

Psalm 146 reads as a summary of duties people in the ancient Near East expected their kings to perform. In the mouth of David, the words become those of a king bowing to the kingship of YHWH and acknowledging the limitations of human rulers.

Interestingly, Psalm 146 appears to be a collection of partial quotations and echoes of other biblical passages. This is a characterization that describes well the nature of the psalms in Books Four and Five of the Psalter, for the shaping community apparently brought together various individual and untitled psalms to shape the last two books of the Psalter. Some were adapted, compiled, or reworked for their new position in the text, but all were authoritative for the shaping community. The psalms in Books Four and Five provide old "tried and true" keys to identity and stability—answers to the question, "What are we to do?"—in a new world situation.

What is the substance, the essence, of the "old truths?" Verse 5 of Psalm 146 begins with אַשְׁרֵי: "Blessed is the one whose help is the God of Jacob." The word אַשְׁרֵי sends the reader/hearer back to Psalms 1 and 2, the beginning of the Psalter, back to the two essentials for the postexilic community—the תורה and the kingship of YHWH.

With Psalm 147, the shaping community broadens the scope of its praise from the individual ancient Israelite represented by David to all of

---

[20]See Gerald H. Wilson, *The Editing of the Hebrew Psalter*, SBLDS 76 (Chico CA: Scholars Press, 1985) 226, and the above discussion of Psalm 145.

Jerusalem. The entire community, not David alone, must join in the praise of YHWH.[21]

> Praise YHWH, O Jerusalem!
> Praise your God, O Zion! (147:12)

Psalm 147 still employs very "kingly" language, emphasizing YHWH's role as king of Israel (vv. 5, 6, 13-15). But, in addition, the reader/hearer encounters creation language in verses 8 and 9, and 16-18:

> Who covers the heavens with clouds,
> Who provides rain for the earth,
> Who makes grass to spring forth on the mountains. (147:8)

Psalm 147 attests clearly the purposeful arrangement of the closing psalms of the Hebrew Psalter. It moves the reader/hearer from an individual praise of the kingship of YHWH to the praise of YHWH by the postexilic Israelite community. The language in Psalm 147 also serves as a bridge between the individual hymn of Psalm 146, which celebrates the "kingly" attributes of YHWH and the creation hymn of Psalm 148, which celebrates YHWH's cosmic works.

Psalm 148 is a creation hymn.[22] The creation language introduced in Psalm 147 is developed fully in Psalm 148, and the reader/hearer is moved one step farther along the succession of praises that close the Psalter. First David, then the people of Zion, and now all of creation is called upon to praise YHWH. Psalms 146, 147, and 148 are purposely placed by the shaping community to "widen the scope" of praise, from the heavens (vv. 1-6) to the earth (vv. 7-13), until it includes even the

> Kings of the earth and all peoples;
> Princes and all judges of the earth;
> Both young men and virgins;
> Old men and children. (148:11-12)

But the scope of praise is widened only to be abruptly narrowed again in verse 14 to the community of YHWH.[23]

> And He has lifted up a horn for His people,

---

[21]Kselman, "Psalm 146 in Its Context," 597.
[22]Bellinger, *Psalms: Reading and Studying the Book of Praises*, 81.
[23]See Hossfeld and Zenger, *Die Psalmen I, Psalm 1–50*, 11.

Praise for all His godly ones;
For the children of Israel, a people near to Him.

Psalm 149 is again directed to Zion, as was Psalm 147. It exhorts the
people to praise YHWH the king [מלך] and YHWH the maker [עשׂה], thus
building upon the language in Psalms 146, 147, and 148. But Psalm 149
is somewhat different and directs the praise of the reader/hearer in a new
direction. Verses 1-5 summon Israel to praise their king and maker in
familiar praise language:

Let Israel be glad in its maker;
Let the children of Zion rejoice in their king.
Let them praise his name with dancing;
Let them sing praises to him with timbrel and lyre. (149:2-3)

Verses 6-9, however, speak of vengeance and judgment. And commentators have long puzzled over the purpose of such language in the
closing הללו־יה psalms of the Psalter. Many have pointed out these verses'
ties to Psalm 2:10-12.[24] Psalm 2 calls upon the nations to "serve YHWH
with fear; with trembling kiss his feet. Lest he become angry and you
perish in the way" (vv. 11, 12). Perhaps Psalm 149 outlines the conse-
quences for those "kings and all peoples, princes and all judges, young
men and virgins, old men and children" (148:11-12) who do not "serve
YHWH with fear."

YHWH is king, but the postexilic community will carry the sword and
execute the vengeance and judgment of YHWH upon the rebellious
nations. That is the promise to those in postexilic Israel who acknowledge YHWH as king and accept the תורה as the way to obedience and
fealty to YHWH the king. "Let the children of Zion rejoice in their king"
(149:2).

Psalm 150 brings the story of the Psalter to a dramatic close. Walter
Brueggemann describes it as "the most extreme and unqualified statement
of unfettered praise in the Old Testament."[25] Each colon of the psalm
contains the familiar הלל summons. And it closes with "Let all that has
breath praise YHWH!"

---

[24]See, e.g., Bellinger, *Psalms: Reading and Studying the Book of Praises*, 8;
and Mays, *Psalms*, 448.
[25]Brueggemann, "Bounded by Obedience and Praise: The Psalms as Canon,"
67.

But this "unfettered" praise is only possible at the *end* of the story of the Psalter. The postexilic community must understand where it has come from (the "Who are we?") and where it is going (the "What are we to do?") before it can participate in the praise of YHWH the king. Thus the Psalter becomes a story of survival in the changed and changing world with which the postexilic Israelite community is confronted.

To understand the story, the reader/hearer must "begin at the beginning" and travel with the Psalter through the history of the nation of ancient Israel. And the reader/hearer must "go on till you come to the end" and find answers to basic questions of existence. The Psalter is deeply imprinted with hermeneutical underpinnings from the community that shaped the text into its final form. And when we ask the question "Why these 150 psalms arranged into these five books?" we find the footprints of the shaping community in every aspect of its structure.

Perhaps the advice given to Rabbi Joshua ben Levi when he tried to arrange the psalms in their proper order was correct: "A heavenly voice came forth and commanded: 'Do not rouse that which slumbers!' "[26] We have shaken the slumbering giant and gained a few sleepy pieces of information. But much remains to be roused!

---

[26]William G. Braude, *The Midrash on Psalms*, vol. 1 (New Haven CT: Yale University Press, 1959) 50.

Chapter 11

The Survival
of the Canonical Community

Introduction

The story of the shaping of the Psalter is the story of the shaping of
survival. The Psalter was, along with the other texts of which the Hebrew
scriptures consist, a constitutive document of identity for postexilic
ancient Israel. Within that collection of texts, the community found a new
structure for existence and identity that transcended traditional concepts
of nationhood. Postexilic Israel had no earthly king and court, only their
temple and cult.[1] The story of the Psalter gave the people a new rationale
for existence, a new statement of national identity. With YHWH as king,
the people could survive as a separate and identifiable entity within the
vast empires—Persian, Greek, and Roman—of which they were a part.

The community shaped the text in order to give itself a rationale for
continued existence, and the text shaped a community that survived the
uncertainties of postexilic existence. In chapter 2 we saw that the final
"shape" of the Psalter probably was not firm until at least the first
century CE. This conclusion fits well with other evidence regarding the
development of the Hebrew canon. At some point in the transmission of
their traditional and authoritative literature, the ancient Israelites determined that certain forms of the text were decisive, and they chose to
make no further updates to them. The texts took on a degree of normative authority, such that subsequent redaction either was thought unnecessary or did not find favor in the community. Can we pinpoint an event

---

[1]And after 70 CE even the temple no longer existed. All that remained was
the cult.

or set of events that would precipitate a move by the ancient Israelites from adhering to a fluid, changing, "updatable," form of scripture to a fixed, unchangeable form? What motivated the community to move from "forming the footprints" to "fixing the footprints"?

The Historical Setting

In the sixth century BCE, the Persian emperor allowed the ancient Israelites in Jerusalem to rebuild their temple and resume their religious practice, but they remained vassals of the Persian state. Temple and cult were restored, but the nation-state which had been ruled by the Davidic dynasty was not. The postexilic community had no real hope of ever having a Davidic king again. It could not look to its monarchy for leadership, stability, and identity. Identity came to be the primary concern of second-temple Judaism. The people questioned two basic issues of existence: "Who is Israel? And what are the rules that define Israel as a social and political entity?"

Ezra and Nehemiah began to provide the postexilic community with answers to these questions. First, the author of the book of Ezra writes that Ezra is greatly disturbed by reports that the Levites, the priests, and the rest of the people of Israel are intermarrying with the Canaanites, the Hittites, the Perizzites, the Jebusites, the Ammonites, the Moabites, the Egyptians, and the Amorites.[2] Ezra prays, confesses, weeps, and prostrates himself before the temple, and the people respond:

> We have been unfaithful to our God, and have married foreign women from the peoples of the land; yet now there is hope for Israel in spite of this. So now let us make a covenant with our God to put away all the wives and their children, according to the counsel of my lord.
>
> (Ezra 10:2b-3 NASV)

Then in the book of Nehemiah, Ezra reads out the law of Moses to a gathering of Israel.[3] The people respond, saying:

> [We are] taking on . . . a curse and an oath to walk in God's Torah, which was given through Moses, God's servant, and to keep and to

---

[2]See Ezra 9:1-2.
[3]See Nehemiah 8:1-8.

observe all the commandments of YHWH our Lord, and His ordinances and His statutes. (Nehemiah 10:29 NASV)

Thus, separation from the surrounding peoples and strict adherence to the Torah of Moses seem to have been two significant keys to maintaining Israel's identity under Persian rule.[4]

At the end of the fourth century BCE, a change of power came to Palestine. Alexander the Great conquered the Persian Empire, established Greek rule over Judea, and introduced Hellenistic culture. We actually know very little about Jewish history during the early part of the Hellenistic period. But Josephus's *The Antiquities of the Jews* indicates that Alexander granted Judaism some status as a legitimate religion.[5] He writes that, on an official visit to Jerusalem, Alexander summoned the Jews before him

and bade them ask what favors they pleased of him: whereupon the high priest desired that they might enjoy the laws of their forefathers, and might pay no tribute on the seventh year. He granted them all that they desired.[6]

---

[4]See also Gösta Ahlström, *The History of Ancient Palestine* (Minneapolis: Fortress Press, 1993) 844-47. Ahlström points out that the problem the authors of Ezra and Nehemiah address is not only a religious one: "It was very much a sociological problem and a problem of property rights" (846).

[5]Scholars differ in their views of the historical veracity of the writings of Josephus. E. P. Sanders, *Judaism: Practice and Belief: 63 B.C.E.–66 C.E.* (Philadelphia: Trinity Press International, 1992) 6, outlines well the attitude with which the "modern historian" must approach the writings of Josephus:

Josephus had his weaknesses and biases, but his general merit as a historian is considerable. . . . Even had Josephus been a worse historian than he was, we would be bound to follow his account of events, since often there is no other. Fortunately, wherever he can be tested, he can be seen to have been a pretty fair historian. [However], a pretty fair historian in the Hellenistic period did not live up to the ideal of disinterested inquiry and objective reporting to which modern historians aspire (but do not fully attain). History was written with a purpose—or two or three.

[6]Flavius Josephus, *The Antiquities of the Jews*, in *The Works of Josephus*, trans. William Whiston (Peabody MA: Hendrickson Publishers, 1987) XI.337-38, 307. Peter Schäfer, "The Hellenistic and Maccabaean Periods," in *Israelite and Judaean History* (London: SCM Press, 1977) 569, points out that it is unlikely that Alexander actually paid a visit to Jerusalem. The high priest of Jerusalem readily submitted, on behalf of all the people, to his rule, so he "left untouched

After the untimely death of Alexander in 323 BCE, Palestine became a sought-after trophy in a power struggle between the Seleucids of Syria and the Ptolemies of Egypt. The Ptolemies held Palestine through most of the third century, but Antiochus III, "the Great," conquered Palestine in 200 BCE. Antiochus III appears to have dealt quite favorably with the Jewish population of Judea. Simon II, the high priest of Jerusalem, sought and obtained Antiochus's favor on behalf of the people.[7] Antiochus issued a decree shortly after conquering Jerusalem in which he stated:

> Since the Jews, upon our first entrance on their country demonstrated their friendship towards us; and when we came to their city, received us in a splendid manner, and came to meet us with their senate, and gave abundance of provisions to our soldiers . . . we have thought fit to reward them, and to retrieve the condition of their city . . . I would also have the work about the temple finished, and the cloisters, and if there be anything else that ought to be rebuilt.[8]

But after the death of Antiochus III and the mysterious disappearance of Simon, the situation quickly deteriorated. Thirty-two years after his assuring decree, Antiochus's son Antiochus IV "Epiphanes" inaugurated ruthless religious controls in Judea, with Jason and then Menelaus as high priests. In 168 BCE, he banned circumcision, observance of the sabbath and holy days, and even the reading of the Torah. In addition, the Jerusalem temple was converted into a pagan sanctuary.[9]

The Jewish people of Judea undoubtedly knew what was taking place in Jerusalem and at the temple. But for the majority of the population, as long as they were able to continue living their own lives as they had in the past, they did not react against the changes. Moreover, a good num-

---

the organizational structure of Judah."
  [7]Schäfer, "The Hellenistic and Maccabaean Periods," 578.
  [8]Josephus, *Antiquities* XII.138-41, 317.
  [9]See James L. Kugel and Rowan A. Greer, *Early Biblical Interpretation* (Philadelphia: Westminster Press, 1986) 43. Much of the motivation for Antiochus IV's actions may have been economic. The Seleucid Empire needed funds to pay tribute to a growing power in the West, Rome. Second Maccabees describes an incident in which the Seleucid king ordered that money in the treasury of the temple at Jerusalem be confiscated as part of the religious controls placed upon Judaism. See 2 Macc 3:4-13.

ber of Jews in Jerusalem were supporters of Jason—who was a member of the hereditary family of high priests—and favored the Hellenization policies of Jason and Antiochus IV.[10]

But the changes did not go entirely unnoticed, and when Menelaus—who was not a member of the hereditary family of high priests—became high priest, circumstances for the Jews worsened.[11] The hellenizing policies finally prompted a rebellion by a group of Jews whose initial goal was to regain their religious freedom and to restore Jewish worship in the temple.[12] Mattathias, a member of the Hasmonean family, led the first revolt against the Seleucids. The author of 1 Maccabees relates Mattathias's speech to a gathering of Jewish rebels:

> Even if all the nations that live under the rule of the king obey him, and have chosen to obey his commandments, everyone of them abandoning the religion of their ancestors, I and my sons and my brothers will continue to live by the covenant of our ancestors. Far be it from us to desert the law and the ordinances. We will not obey the king's words by turning aside from our religion to the right hand or to the left.
>
> (2:19-22 NRSV)[13]

---

[10]Otto Morkholm, "Antiochus IV," in *The Cambridge History of Judaism*, vol. 2, ed. W. D. Davies and Louis Finkelstein (Cambridge: Cambridge University Press, 1989) 281. Morkholm writes:

> It appears clearly that many Jews of the time, also among the priests, felt attracted by Hellenistic culture and were eager to acquire a formal Greek education in order to place themselves on an equal footing with neighbouring peoples and overcome the isolation into which the orthodox followers of the Torah constrained themselves. To these people the strict Jewish separatism meant material and spiritual poverty to the whole nation.

[11]See ibid., 281-87, for a comprehensive treatment of the time of Menelaus.

[12]Shaye J. D. Cohen, in "The Political and Social History of the Jews in Greco-Roman Antiquity: The State of the Question," in *Early Judaism and Its Modern Interpreters*, The Bible and Its Modern Interpreters 2, ed. Robert A. Kraft and Geroge W. E. Nickelsburg (Philadelphia: Fortress Press, 1986) 42-43, states that in the second century BCE revolts and riots were common not only in Judea but also in Egypt, Persia, and elsewhere. "The slogan of these movements was hatred of the Greeks and Hellenism." Cohen's observations remind us that issues of religion, politics, and economics were difficult to separate in this period and thus we should not put too great a "religious" emphasis upon the motivations of the Hasmoneans.

[13]Schäfer, "The Hellenistic and Maccabaean Periods," 585, maintains that the

The Jews quickly achieved their goals. In 164 BCE, Antiochus V, the son of Antiochus IV, wrote a letter that is preserved in 2 Maccabees:

> We have heard that the Jews do not consent to our father's change to Greek customs, but prefer their own way of living and ask that their own customs be allowed them. Accordingly, since we choose that this nation also should be free from disturbance, our decision is that their temple be restored to them and that they shall live according to the customs of their ancestors. (11:24-25 NRSV)

The next goal of the Jewish rebels was complete political independence from the Seleucid empire. Only a self-governing nation-state, they deemed, would give them a full restoration of identity and hope for the future. The Hasmoneans obtained Roman support for their endeavor in 161 BCE, since Rome was interested in weakening Syrian hold on the East.[14]

> The decree of the senate concerning a league of assistance and friendship with the nation of the Jews. It shall not be lawful for any that are subject to the Romans to make war with the nation of the Jews, nor to assist those that do so, either by sending them corn, or ships, or money; and if any attack be made upon the Jews, the Romans shall assist them. . . .[15]

The pact with Rome and the growing disintegration of the Seleucid monarchy permitted the Hasmoneans to establish an independent Jewish state by 141 BCE. The Jews made Simon, the last surviving son of Mattathias, leader and high priest "until a trustworthy prophet should arise" (1 Maccabees 14:35). The seemingly provisional nature of Simon's appointment can be attributed to a certain amount of opposition in Jerusalem to Hasmonean rule. Not all Jews had supported the actions of the rebels. In fact, during this period a number of distinct groups and sects formed within the Jewish community.

---

account in Maccabees is a "tendentious but still essentially historical" account. The authors of Maccabees, like Josephus, had a bias in their view of the events of the period.

[14]Ibid., 589.

[15]Josephus, *Antiquities* XII.417-19, 334. See also 1 Maccabees 8:17-30.

The dubious reigns of Alexander Jannaeus (103-76 BCE) and his wife Alexandra Salome (76-67 BCE) marked the end of the Hasmonean Dynasty and a short-lived independent Jewish state. The Roman general Pompey conquered Jerusalem in the late autumn of 63 BCE and brought Palestine under the rule of Rome. The years of independence, though short, made a lasting impact on ancient Judaism. The long hoped-for restoration of an Israelite nation proved to be only a passing phenomenon. The world had not been set aright. Judaism was again under the thumb of a foreign power, and the people were once again faced with the old questions of identity and survival.

At the beginning of its occupation of Palestine, Rome recognized Judaism as a legitimate religion and was happy to allow the Jews a degree of self-rule. Josephus records a lengthy decree by Julius Caesar assuring the Jews religious autonomy.[16] A reinstated Hyrcanus II served as high priest and ethnarch from 63 to 40 BCE. In 37 BCE, Herod the Great was crowned king of Judea. The tyrannical nature of Herod's reign—which spawned much social and political unrest—was its lasting legacy to the history of Judaism. When Herod died in 4 BCE, the Jews begged Rome to allow Jerusalem to become a Roman province and be governed directly from Rome. Instead, Herod's handpicked successor Archelaus became ethnarch of Judea.[17] Within ten years, he was ousted from office, and the Jews got their wish for direct Roman rule.

Initially this arrangement seemed to restore some tranquility to the land, but before long relations between the Jews and the Roman authorities deteriorated. The days of Pontius Pilate and Gaius Caligula were especially tense. Josephus writes about a Roman official named Gessius Florus that

> he was the most barbarous; and in things of the greatest turpitude, he was most impudent; nor could anyone outdo him in disguising the truth; nor could anyone contrive more subtle ways of deceit than he did.[18]

Tensions grew until the Roman emperor Nero appointed Titus Flavius Vespasian, one of Rome's leading generals, to regain control of Palestine. Vespasian proceeded cautiously, conquering Galilee in 67 CE and most

---

[16]See Josephus, *Antiquities* XIV.190-222, 378.
[17]See Josephus, *Antiquities* XVII.224-47, and *The Wars of the Jews* II.20-36.
[18]Josephus, *The Wars of the Jews* II.278, 615.

of Judea in 68 CE. Nero died in 68, Vespasian was made emperor, and Vespasian's son Titus completed the siege of Jerusalem. The temple itself was destroyed on the ninth and tenth of Av, 70 CE.[19]

The Shaping of the Canon

The first-century destruction of the temple is a watershed event in the history of Judaism. In the decades that followed, the Hebrew canon of scripture, the synagogue, and rabbinic Judaism rapidly developed, shaping the Jewish religion into the form with which we are familiar. Why was this single event so important? Jacob Neusner suggests:

> What was important was not that the Temple was destroyed; that had happened not once but many times before. It was that the Temple was not then rebuilt.[20]

And, as if to confirm this fact once and for all, sixty-five years after Titus destroyed the temple, a Jewish army under the leadership of Bar Kochba made one last attempt to regain Jerusalem and the temple. They suffered total defeat at the hands of the Romans.

Ancient Israel had already lost king and court. Now the last remaining source of national identity—the temple—was gone as well. The implications for the future of Judaism were enormous. Thus Neusner is correct, but only partially correct. Another problem confronted Judaism, namely, Christianity.

Just before and during the days of the independent Jewish state which the Hasmoneans established in the late second century, BCE, a number of distinct groups emerged within Judaism. The Sadducees, the Pharisees, the Essenes, the Hasidim, the Zealots, and others played important roles in the shaping of Judaism as it entered the Common Era and sorted out its position within the Roman Empire. An important legacy of these groups is the literature they produced, including the writings now labeled as the Apocrypha, the Pseudepigrapha, the Dead Sea Scrolls, the

---

[19]For an analysis of the background of the Roman destruction of Jerusalem, see Thomas A. Idinopulos, "Religious and National Factors in Israel's War with Rome," in *Jewish Civilization in the Hellenistic-Roman Period*, JSPSup 10 (Sheffield: JSOT Press, 1991) 50-63.

[20]Jacob Neusner, *Judaism in the Beginning of Christianity* (Philadelphia: Fortress Press, 1984) 43-44.

Elephantine Papyri, and the Tanaitic (Pharisaic) literature. From this literature, we gain insight into the mindset of the participants in this critical era of Jewish history.

Another significant movement that emerged out of Judaism during this time was Christianity. It began as a part of Judaism and, during the first few decades of its existence, functioned largely within Judaism—including participating in the cultic ceremonies at the temple. The point at which Christians differed from their Jewish counterparts was their interpretation of the Torah.[21] The Christian concept of Torah, combined with a strong eschatological faith, produced a theology that proved to be a serious internal threat to Jewish beliefs and identity.

At perhaps the most volatile point in the history of ancient Judaism, a group emerged from within Israel and claimed that they were the recipients of the ultimate fulfillment of the Torah. James Sanders writes:

> Nobody succeeded in adding a chapter to the basic Torah story until the New Testament. . . . [The Christians made a] quite bold and scandalous claim that in Christ God committed another salvation or righteousness and that it should be added to the Torah story as a climax, as the ultimate chapter of the whole story.[22]

Ancient Judaism was already struggling for survival in the wake of Roman governmental controls and for identity in the face of Christian religious challenges when the temple was destroyed in 70 CE. But we *can* say that the destruction of the temple was a decisive moment in the history of Judaism.

When Rome destroyed the temple, only two groups within Judaism survived—the Pharisees, who formed what we know as rabbinic Judaism, and the Christians of the early church. Each group claimed to be the true heir of ancient Israel. Each offered an all-encompassing interpretation of scripture. Each promised salvation for individuals and for Israel as a whole. And each group had to attempt to make some sense of what had happened and to develop a system for worshiping God without the temple

---

[21]Judaism in the first century stressed what James Sanders calls the "ethos"—the instruction—aspect of the Torah, while Christianity emphasized the "mythos"—the story—aspect. See James Sanders, "Torah and Christ," in *From Sacred Story to Sacred Text* (Philadelphia: Fortress Press, 1987) 44.

[22]Ibid., 51-52.

at Jerusalem. Jacob Neusner points out that wherever the rabbis and their opinions succeeded, Christians and their views did not. And wherever the Christians were successful, the rabbis were not.[23]

Many in the early Church viewed the destruction of the temple as a punishment for the people—the Jews—who had rejected Jesus and thus as a final vindication of the Christian faith. Eusebius suggested that

> Those who believed in Christ migrated from Jerusalem, so when holy men had altogether deserted the royal capital of the Jews . . . the judgment of God might at last overtake them for all their crimes against Christ and his apostles, and all that generation of the wicked be utterly blotted out from among men. . . . Such was the reward of the iniquity of the Jews and of their impiety against the Christ of God.[24]

The leaders of the Christians went boldly forward, convinced of their claim to be the true Israel.

But the leaders of the Jews did not give up after the destruction of the temple. Under the leadership of Rabban Yohanan ben Zakkai, rabbinic Judaism moved from Jerusalem to Yavneh (Jamnia), a town on the coast of Palestine due west of Jerusalem, where it established a new Sanhedrin and scribal school. Judaism needed a stable base of identity, and it needed a mechanism for adaptability to its new situation. For, while stability is vital to survival, so is adaptability.

In the centuries between the fall of the first temple in 586 BCE and the fall of the second temple in 70 CE, the ancient Israelites had been moving toward putting their traditional and authoritative literature into a fixed form. By the first century CE, they possessed a fairly well-defined body of scripture which included the Torah, the Prophets, and some form of the Writings.[25] Rabbinic legend maintains that over the course of several decades the scribes at Yavneh completed the process of fixing the form of the Hebrew scriptures.[26]

---

[23]Jacob Neusner, *First Century Judaism in Crisis* (Nashville: Abingdon Press, 1975) 39-40.

[24]Eusebius, *Ecclesiastical History*, quoted in Neusner, *Judaism in the Beginning of Christianity*, 91.

[25]I base my statement on the evidence from Josephus, Ben Sirach, Qumran, and various New Testament passages. See above, chapter 2.

[26]Jack P. Lewis, "Council of Jamnia (Jabneh)," in *Anchor Bible Dictionary*, vol. 3 (New York: Doubleday, 1992) 634, reminds us that we cannot view the

In the traditional story, the rabbinic leaders, "seventy-two elders" according to *m. Yadayim* 3:5 (in the Mishnah), made a final decision on the literature that would be included in the Hebrew scriptures.[27] The "Five Books of Moses" (the Torah), all but one book of the Prophets (Joshua through the Twelve), and the Psalms—in some form—already were accepted as scripture by the larger Jewish community. Five books— Ezekiel, Proverbs, Ecclesiastes, the Song of Songs, and Esther—were examined by the group at Yavneh. The focus of the discussion on each book revolved around one of two issues: whether the book "made the hands unclean," or whether the book "should be stored away."

In order to "make the hands unclean," a book must contain a text "spoken by the Holy Spirit"[28] and must be written in the Hebrew or Aramaic language, in square script, on parchment and in ink.[29] A book that "made the hands unclean" was "stored away" in a geniza (a repository in a synagogue) either when it was too worn out to be used

---

goings-on at Javneh as a "council of Javneh." He writes:

> In short, the Council of Jamnia . . . is, in the absence of attestation in specific texts, used in scholarship as a convenient symbol for the culmination of long processes in early Judaism. Sometimes used for any development between A.D. 70 and 135, the terminology has the disadvantage of inviting the uninformed to assume official action taken at specific meetings on specific dates.

[27]Roger T. Beckwith, "Formation of the Hebrew Bible," in *Mikra: Text, Translation, Reading, and Interpretation of the Hebrew Bible in Ancient Judaism and Early Christianity*, ed. Martin Jan Mulder (Philadelphia: Fortress Press, 1988) 58.

[28]Tosefta *Yadayim* 2:14 states: "Rabban Simeon b. Menassia says: 'The Song of Songs imparts uncleanness to hands, because it was said by the Holy Spirit. Qohelet does not impart uncleanness of hands, because it is [merely] the wisdom of Solomon.' "

[29]Mishnah *Yadayim* 4:5 states:

> The [Aramaic] version that is in Ezra and Daniel renders the hands unclean. If an [Aramaic] version [contained in the Scriptures] was written in [archaic] Hebrew, or if [Scripture that is in] Hebrew was written in an [Aramaic] version, or in [Archaic] Hebrew script, it does not render the hands unclean. [The Scriptures] render the hands unclean only if they are written in Assyrian (square Hebrew) characters, on leather, and in ink.

any longer or if it caused such serious interpretational problems that it was better for it to perish than to be read.[30]

The Yavneh rabbis discussed whether to "store away" Ezekiel and Proverbs, whether Esther "made the hands unclean," and both issues in regard to Ecclesiastes and the Song of Songs.[31] However, the group at Yavneh did not make any "new" rulings about the status of the five books in question. The books formed, along with the rest of the Torah, the Prophets, and the Writings, the traditional and authoritative "canon" of the postexilic community. The discussions at Yavneh could only reflect what was already happening in the Jewish community.[32]

Yavneh's role in stabilizing the Hebrew "canon" was probably that of finally laying to rest questions about the status of any books that, though accepted as scripture, had been the subject of discussion in Pharisaic circles before 70 CE, including any questions about different "editions" of scriptural books, including the Psalter. At this time the community addressed any remaining questions about the shaping of the Psalter—especially in Books Four and Five—and determined a "final" form of the text.[33] Too much was at stake at this point in Judaism's history. The footprints had to be fixed or they might fade into the quagmire of change surrounding ancient Judaism. Stability became increasingly important.

Maintaining Adaptability

Adaptability was also an important characteristic of postexilic Judaism. Fortunately, a system of religious adaptability was already in place in the first century CE. Pharisaic tradition maintained that at Sinai, YHWH gave Moses two forms of the Torah—the Written and the Oral. The Oral

---

[30]See Beckwith, "Formation of the Hebrew Bible," 61-68.

[31]For full records of the discussions, see Babylonian Talmud *Shabbat* 30b, *Avot de-Rabban Natan* A1, 2, Mishnah *Eduyot* 5:3, Mishnah *Yadayim* 3:5, and Tosefta *Yadayim* 2:14.

[32]James A. Sanders, *Canon and Community: A Guide to Canonical Criticism*, GBS (Philadelphia: Fortress Press, 1984) 11.

[33]In my discussion above, in chapter 4, I argue that Books Four and Five have a different and later editorial history than Books One, Two, and Three. And I discuss the wisdom influences (more prevalent in the late postexilic community) within Books Four and Five. Based upon this evidence, I posit that it is quite reasonable to argue that the Psalter received its final, fixed shape at Yavneh.

Torah was passed down along with the Written Torah, and while the Written Torah became more and more fixed in form, the Oral Torah remained fluid, providing interpretations of the Written Torah for new situations in the life of ancient Israel.[34]

During the second century CE, the rabbinic leaders preserved the Oral Torah in writing. The Mishnah, as the written version of the Oral Torah is called, contains some four centuries of Palestinian Pharisaic religious and cultural activity, beginning in the early second century BCE and ending in the late second century CE. Why was the Oral Torah put into writing? Apparently it was done for the same reason that the Written Torah was preserved in a fixed form. The Tosefta *Eduyot*, a supplement to the Mishnah *Eduyot*, states:

> When sages came together in the vineyard at Yavneh, they said, "The time is coming at which a person will go looking for a teaching of Torah and will not find it, a teaching of the scribes and will not find it. . . . " They said, "Let us begin from Hillel and from Shammai."[35]

Another important issue for post-second-temple Judaism was how it would carry out cultic functions without the temple. Here, also, stability and adaptability are the key ingredients. According to the ruling of the rabbinic leaders, customs and rites would remain the same in outward form, but those activities once performed only at the temple in Jerusalem would now be decentralized and performed in synagogues throughout the land. How did the rabbinic leaders justify this move? The Mishnah *Rosh ha-Shanah* states:

> Beforetime the *Lulab* [the festive palm branch of Sukkoth] was carried seven days in the Temple, but in the provinces one day only. After the Temple was destroyed, Rabban Yohanan ben Zakkai ordained that in the provinces it should be carried seven days in memory of the Temple.[36]

---

[34]See Rimon Kasher, "Scripture in Rabbinic Literature," in *Mikra: Text, Translation, Reading, and Interpretation of the Hebrew Bible in Ancient Judaism and Early Christianity*, 548-53.

[35]See Tosefta *Eduyot* 1:1.

[36]See Mishnah *Rosh ha-Shanah* 4:3.

Thus the "memory of the temple" was the rationale given to the Jewish people for continuing to perform important community functions in new worship situations. Rabbinic Judaism proved over and over to be masterful at achieving both stability and adaptability.

The story of the Psalter demonstrates too the stability and adaptability of early Judaism. The stability for the people was the memory of David, YHWH's chosen king, and the "golden age" of the nation of Israel. Their adaptability came in acknowledging YHWH as king so that they could remain an identifiable entity within the Persian, Greek, and Roman empires of which they were a part.

Chapter 12

The Psalter at Work
in the Community of Faith

In *Introduction to the Old Testament as Scripture*, Brevard Childs asks, "In what way does the final editing of the Psalter testify as to how the collectors understood the canonical material to function for the community of faith?"[1] The collectors—the postexilic community—used the traditional cult material of ancient Israel to construct a popular expression of confidence in a new existential rationale for existence. But are we justified in arguing that the Psalter, the so-called "hymnbook of the second temple," could be shaped into a seemingly "political" document? Did the shaping community have the freedom to manipulate the text in such a way?

The canonical Psalter represents only a small selection of the total number of psalms in circulation in postexilic Israel. Through a long process of use and selection, certain individual psalms and collections of psalms gained popularity and became part of the corporate tradition of the people—that is, they became normative and authoritative. The Psalter was not an original and innovative piece of literature. The community that shaped it into its final form simply finished a process that had been going on for centuries. The content of the Psalter was familiar to the cultic community. Only its external form was new, determined by the exigencies of postexilic life.

What perception did the Israelite community have of the shape of the Psalter? The Psalter's external shape was that of a constitutive charter of existence for the postexilic community, but its internal form was that of

---

[1]Brevard S. Childs, *Introduction to the Old Testament as Scripture* (Philadelphia: Fortress Press, 1979) 512-13.

traditional cultic material. The canonical Psalter exercised a dual role in the life of the community. Individual psalms and collections of psalms were still used at ceremonies and festivals.[2] But the Psalter as a whole was read publicly[3] to remind the Israelites of a story—the story of the majestic reign of King David, the dark days of oppression and exile, the restoration of the glorious reign of YHWH, and the surety that Israel could continue to exist as a "nation" in the ancient Near East.

Both uses of the psalms were important to the ongoing life of the postexilic community and worked together in a reciprocal relationship. Their liturgical (or cultic) use influenced the meaning and significance of the psalms in their canonical (or constitutive) context, and their canonical use influenced the meaning and significance of the psalms in their cultic context.[4] In summary, the Psalter provided a meaningful rationale for the postexilic community to continue to strive for individuality and recognition as a separate entity within the empires by which it was ruled continually from the time of the Babylonian conquest in 586 BCE.

---

[2] 2 Chronicles 20-36, Mishnah Tamid 7:4, and Psalms 120–134 mention the use of psalms in various worship, ceremony, and festival settings. And the Talmud mentions that psalms were part of the temple services for New Moon, Rosh Hashanah, and Sukkoth. See Simon Cohen, "Liturgical Psalms," in *Universal Jewish Encyclopedia*, ed. Isaac Landman et al. (New York: Universal Jewish Encyclopedia Co., 1943) 9:18-19.

[3] Gerald H. Wilson, in *The Editing of the Hebrew Psalter*, SBLDS 76 (Chico CA: Scholars Press, 1985) 207, maintains that the canonical Psalter was no longer simply a collection of cultic hymns, but that it was now a book "to be read rather than performed, meditated over rather than recited from." But in the ancient Near East, literary texts were not read individually, but out loud before groups of listeners, since few people in the ancient Near East were literate. See Aaron Demsky and Meir Bar-Ilan, "Writing in Ancient Israel and Early Judaism," in *Mikra: Text, Translation, Reading, and Interpretation of the Hebrew Bible in Ancient Judaism and Early Christianity*, ed. Martin Jan Mulder (Philadelphia: Fortress Press, 1988) 10-16.

[4] I argue a dual function for the Psalter against Wilson, who maintains that the Psalter could not have been used for "individual meditation and prayer" at a time when it was still used in "cultic celebration," and that the Psalter still could not have been used in the cult at a time when it was used for "individual meditation and prayer." See Gerald H. Wilson, "A First Century CE Date for the Closing of the Hebrew Psalter?" in *Haim M. I. Gevaryahu Memorial Volume*, ed. Joshua J. Adler (Jerusalem: World Jewish Bible Center, 1990) 42.

Conclusion

In the introduction to *The Intellectual Adventure of Ancient Man: An Essay on Speculative Thought in the Ancient Near East*, Henri Frankfort and H. A. Frankfort discuss myth in the ancient Near East as the result of the search by humankind for "intellectually satisfying" answers to basic questions of existence, questions such as, "How did my world come into being?" "How do the gods affect what happens to me?" "Has life always been the way it is?" "Will it always remain the same?" The Frankforts call the process of arriving at answers to these questions "speculative thought." They observe:

> We may say that speculative thought attempts to underpin the chaos of experience so that it may reveal the features of a structure—order, coherence, and meaning.[5]

In ancient Mesopotamia, the rainstorm that ended a drought was not explained as resulting from a change in certain atmospheric conditions. Rather, the giant bird god Anzu devoured the Bull of Heaven, whose hot breath had scorched the land, and then spread its wings over the sky to form the black rain clouds. Mesopotamian society fulfilled its need to structure the phenomenal world by personifying natural forces as gods. The intervention of Anzu was an "intellectually satisfying," if numinous, explanation for the coming of rain to end a drought.

In the same way, Israel survived because the postexilic community found an "intellectually satisfying" rationale for survival. As Anzu was an "intellectually satisfying" rationale for the rains that ended the drought in ancient Mesopotamia, so YHWH as king was an "intellectually satisfying" rationale for the continued existence of the nation of ancient Israel. The postexilic community had indeed found a way to "underpin the chaos of experience [and] reveal the features of a structure—order, coherence, and meaning."[6]

The postexilic community found a new structure for existence and identity by redefining "nationhood" in the context of its culture in the an-

---

[5]Henri Frankfort, H. A. Frankfort, John A. Wilson, Thorkild Jacobsen, and William A. Irwin, *The Intellectual Adventure of Ancient Man* (Chicago: University of Chicago Press, 1977) 3.

[6]Ibid.

cient Near East. King, court, and temple were gone, but Israel survived. Israel survived because it appropriated and shaped its traditional and cultic material into a constitutive document of identity, the Hebrew scriptures. And the Psalter is a part of that constitutive document.

"Begin at the beginning . . . and go on until you come to the end." The instruction of the befuddled King of Hearts is where this study began, and where it ends. By beginning at the beginning of the Psalter and going on until we come to the end, we readers discover that YHWH *is* king, regardless of the external exigencies of life. That affirmation was central to the survival and future of the postexilic community of Israel and remains central to the survival and future of the believing community today. YHWH is king. הללו־יה!

Bibliography

Ahlström, Gösta W. *The History of Ancient Palestine*. Minneapolis: Fortress Press, 1993.

Albright, William F. "A Catalogue of Early Hebrew Lyric Poems (Ps. LXVIII)." *Hebrew Union College Annual* 23 (1950): 1-40.

Allen, Leslie C. *Psalms 101–150*. Word Biblical Commentary 21. Waco TX: Word Books, 1983.

Anderson, A. A. *The Book of Psalms*. Two volumes. New Century Bible. Grand Rapids MI: Eerdmans Publishing Co., 1972.

Barr, James. "Childs' *Introduction to the Old Testament as Scripture*." *Journal for the Study of the Old Testament* 16 (1980): 12-23.

_____. *Comparative Philology and the Text of the Old Testament*. Oxford: SCM Press, 1968.

Barton, John. *Oracles of God: Perceptions of Ancient Prophecy in Israel After the Exile*. London: Darton, Longman, and Todd, 1986.

_____. *Reading the Old Testament*. Philadelphia: Westminster Press, 1984.

Becker, J. *Urform und Neuinterpretation in den Psalmen*. Stuttgart: Katholisches Bibelwerk, 1966.

Beckwith, Roger T. "Formation of the Hebrew Bible." In *Mikra: Text, Translation, Reading and Interpretation of the Hebrew Bible in Ancient Judaism and Early Christianity*, edited by Martin Jan Mulder, 39-86. Philadelphia: Fortress Press, 1988.

Bellinger, William H., Jr. *Psalmody and Prophecy*. Journal for the Study of the Old Testament Supplement Series 27. Sheffield UK: JSOT Press, 1984.

_____. *Psalms: Reading and Studying the Book of Praises*. Peabody MA: Hendrickson Publishers, 1990.

Beyerlin, Walter. *Werden und Wesen des 107 Psalms*. Berlin: Walter de Gruyter, 1979.

Blenkinsopp, Joseph. *Prophecy and Canon*. Notre Dame IN: University of Notre Dame Press, 1977.

_____. *Wisdom and Law in the Old Testament*. Oxford: Oxford University Press, 1983.

Braude, William G. *The Midrash on Psalms*. Two volumes. New Haven CT: Yale University Press, 1959.

Briggs, Charles Augustus, and Emilie Grace Briggs. *A Critical and Exegetical Commentary on the Book of Psalms.* Two volumes. International Critical Commentary. Edinburgh: T.&T. Clark; New York: Charles Scribner's Sons, 1906.

Bright, John. *A History of Israel.* Third edition. Philadelphia: Westminster Press, 1981.

Brooke, George J. *Exegesis at Qumran: 4QFlorilegium in its Jewish Context.* Journal for the Study of the Old Testament Supplement Series 29. Sheffield UK: JSOT Press, 1985.

Brueggemann, Walter. "Bounded by Obedience and Praise: The Psalms as Canon." *Journal for the Study of the Old Testament* 50 (1991): 63-92.

_____. *Israel's Praise: Doxology against Idolatry and Ideology.* Philadelphia: Fortress Press, 1988.

_____. *The Message of the Psalms: A Theological Commentary.* Ausburg Old Testament Studies. Minneapolis: Augsburg Publishing House, 1984.

Buber, Martin. "The Heart Determines: Psalm 73." In *Theodicy in the Old Testament,* edited by James L. Crenshaw, 109-18. Philadelphia: Fortress Press, 1983.

Carroll, Lewis. *Alice in Wonderland.* Second edition. A Norton Critical Edition. Edited by Donald J. Gray. New York: W. W. Norton and Co., 1992.

Cazelles, Henri. אַשְׁרֵי *'ashrê.* In *Theological Dictionary of the Old Testament,* volume 1, edited by G. Johannes Botterweck and Helmer Ringgren, translated by John T. Willis, 445-48. Grand Rapids MI: Eerdmans Publishing Co., 1974.

Ceresko, Anthony R. "The Sage in the Psalms." In *The Sage in Israel and the Ancient Near East,* edited by John G. Gammie and Leo G. Perdue, 217-30. Winona Lake IN: Eisenbrauns, 1990.

Childs, Brevard S. *Biblical Theology in Crisis.* Philadelphia: Westminster Press, 1970.

_____. *Introduction to the Old Testament as Scripture.* Philadelphia: Fortress Press, 1979.

_____. "Psalm Titles and Midrashic Exegesis." *Journal of Semitic Studies* 16 (1971): 137-50.

_____. "Reflections on the Modern Study of the Psalms." In *Magnalia Dei: The Mighty Acts of God,* edited by Frank M. Cross, Werner E. Lemke, and Patrick D. Miller, Jr., 377-88. Garden City NY: Doubleday, 1976.

_____. "Response to Reviews of *Introduction to the Old Testament as Scripture.*" *Journal for the Study of the Old Testament* 16 (1980): 52-60.

Clements, Ronald E. *One Hundred Years of Old Testament Interpretation.* Philadelphia: Westminster Press, 1976.

_____. *Wisdom in Theology.* The Didsbury Lectures. Grand Rapids MI: Eerdmans Publishing Co., 1992.

Clines, David J. A. "Psalms Research Since 1955. II. The Literary Genres." *The Tyndale Bulletin* 20 (1969): 103-25.

Cohen, Shaye J. D. "The Political and Social History of the Jews in Greco-Roman Antiquity: The State of the Question." In *Early Judaism and its Modern Interpreters*, 33-56. The Bible and Its Modern Interpreters 2. Philadelphia: Fortress Press, 1986.

Cohen, Simon. "Liturgical Psalms." In *Universal Jewish Encyclopedia*, vol. 9, edited by Isaac Landman et al., 18-19. New York: Universal Jewish Encyclopedia Co., 1943.

Collins, Terence. "Decoding the Psalms: A Structural Approach to the Psalter." *Journal for the Study of the Old Testament* 37 (1987): 41-60.

Coote, Robert B., and Keith W. Whitelam. *The Emergence of Early Israel in Historical Perspective*. Sheffield UK: Almond Press, 1987.

Craigie, Peter C. *Psalms 1–50*. Word Biblical Commentary 19. Waco TX: Word Books, 1983.

Crenshaw, James L. *Old Testament Wisdom. An Introduction*. Atlanta: John Knox Press, 1981.

Dahood, Mitchell, S. J. *Psalms I: 1–50, Psalms II: 51–100*, and *Psalms III: 101–150*. The Anchor Bible 16, 17, and 18. Garden City NY: Doubleday, 1966, 1968, and 1970.

Dalley, Stephanie. *Myths from Mesopotamia: Creation, The Flood, Gilgamesh and Others*. Oxford: Oxford University Press, 1989.

Danby, Herbert. *The Mishnah*. Oxford: Oxford University Press, 1958.

Davies, Philip R. *In Search of "Ancient Israel"*. Journal for the Study of the Old Testament Supplement Series 148. Sheffield UK: Sheffield Academic Press, 1992.

Deimel, A. *Codex Hammurabi*. Rome: Pontifical Biblical Institute, 1950.

Demsky, Aaron, and Meir Bar-Ilan. "Writing in Ancient Israel and Early Judaism." In *Mikra: Text, Translation, Reading and Interpretation of the Hebrew Bible in Ancient Judaism and Early Christianity*, edited by Martin Jan Mulder, 1-38. Philadelphia: Fortress Press, 1988.

Driver, S. R. *Introduction to the Literature of the Old Testament*. Ninth edition. New York: Charles Scribners' Sons, 1913.

Duhm, Bernard. *Die Psalmen*. Kurzer Hand-Kommentar zum Alten Testament. Tübingen: J. C. B. Mohr (Paul Siebeck), 1922.

Eaton, John H. *Kingship and the Psalms*. Second edition. Sheffield UK: JSOT Press, 1986.

Ellis, E. Earle. "The Old Testament Canon in the Early Church." In *Mikra: Text, Translation, Reading and Interpretation of the Hebrew Bible in Ancient Judaism and Early Christianity*, edited by Martin Jan Mulder, 653-90. Philadelphia: Fortress Press, 1988.

Epstein, Isidore, ed. *The Babylonian Talmud: Berakoth*. Translated by Maurice Simon. London: Soncino Press, 1958.

Ewald, G. H. A. V. *Commentary on the Psalms*. Two volumes. Translated by E. Johnson. London: Williams and Norgate, 1880.

Fitzmyer, Joseph A. *The Dead Sea Scrolls: Major Publications and Tools for Study*. Missoula MT: Scholars Press, 1975.

Flint, Peter W. *The Psalters in the Scrolls and the Book of Psalms*. Studies on the Texts of the Desert of Judah Series. Leiden: E. J. Brill, 1995.

Frankfort, Henri. *Kingship and the Gods*. Chicago: University of Chicago Press, 1978.

_____, H. A. Frankfort, John A. Wilson, Thorkild Jacobsen, and William F. Irwin. *The Intellectual Adventure of Ancient Man*. Chicago: University of Chicago Press, 1977.

Freedman, David N. "Archaic Forms in Early Hebrew Poetry." *Zeitschrift für die alttestamentliche Wissenschaft* 72 (1960): 101-107.

_____. "Other than Moses . . . Who Asks (or Tells) God to Repent?" *Bible Review* 1/4 (1985): 56-59.

Gafni, Isaiah. "Historical Background." In *Jewish Writings of the Second Temple Period: Apocrypha, Pseudepigrapha, Qumran Sectarian Writings, Philo, and Josephus*. Edited by Michael E. Stone. Philadelphia: Fortress Press, 1984.

Gammie, John G., and Leo G. Perdue, ed. *The Sage in Israel and the Ancient Near East*. Winona Lake IN: Eisenbrauns, 1990.

Garbini, Giovanni. *History and Ideology in Ancient Israel*. London: SCM Press, 1986.

Gerstenberger, Erhard S. "Der Psalter als Buch und als Sammlung." In *Neue Wege der Psalmenforschung: für Walter Beyerlin*, edited by Klaus Seybold and Erich Zenger, 3-13. Freiburg: Herder, 1994.

_____. *Psalms: Part I, with an Introduction to Cultic Poetry*. The Forms of Old Testament Literature 14. Grand Rapids MI: Eerdmans Publishing Co., 1988.

_____. "Psalms." In *Old Testament Form Criticism*, Trininty University Monograph Series in Religion 2. San Antonio: Trinity University Press, 1974.

Ginsberg, H. L. "A Phoenician Hymn in the Psalter," *Atti del XIX Congresso Internazionale degli Orientalisti*, 472-76. Rome: 1935.

Goulder, Michael D. "The Fourth Book of the Psalter." *Journal of Theological Studies* 26 (1975): 269-89.

_____. *The Psalms of the Sons of Korah*. Journal for the Study of the Old Testament Supplement Series 20. Sheffield UK: Sheffield Academic Press, 1982.

Greenstein, Edward L. "On the Prefixed Preterite in Biblical Hebrew." *Hebrew Studies* 29 (1988): 7-17.

Gunkel, Hermann. *Die Psalmen*. Göttingen: Vandenhoeck & Ruprecht, 1929.

_____. *The Psalms: A Form-Critical Introduction*. Translated by Thomas M. Horner. Facet Books Biblical Series 19. Philadelphia: Fortress Press, 1967.

_____ and Joachim Begrich. *Einleitung in die Psalmen*. Göttingen: Vandenhoeck Ruprecht, 1933.

Hengstenberg, E. W. *Commentary on the Psalms*. Fourth edition. Edinburgh: T.&T. Clark, 1867.

Herrmann, Siegfried. *A History of Israel in Old Testament Times*. Philadelphia: Fortress Press, 1981.

Holladay, William L. "A New Proposal for the Crux in Psalm II 12." *Vetus Testamentum* 28 (1978): 110-12.

_____. *The Psalms through Three Thousand Years: Prayerbook of a Cloud of Witnesses*. Minneapolis: Fortress Press, 1993.

Hossfeld, Frank-Lothar, and Erich Zenger. *Die Psalmen I, Psalm 1–50*. Die Neue Echter Bibel: Kommentar zum Alten Testament mit dem Einheitsübersetzung. Würzburg: Echter Verlag, 1993.

Huehnergard, John. "The Early Hebrew Prefix-Conjugations." *Hebrew Studies* 29 (1988): 19-23.

Idinopulos, Thomas A. "Religious and National Factors in Israel's War with Rome." In *Jewish Civilization in the Hellenistic-Roman Period*, Journal for the Study of the Pseudepigrapha Supplement Series 10, edited by Shemaryahu Talmon, 50-63. Sheffield UK: JSOT Press, 1991.

Jacobsen, Thorkild. *Treasures of Darkness*. New Haven CT: Yale University Press, 1976.

_____. *The Sumerian King List*. Assyrian Studies 11. Chicago: University of Chicago Press, 1939.

Johnson, A. R. "The Psalms." In *The Old Testament and Modern Study*. Edited by H. H. Rowley. Oxford: Clarendon Press, 1951.

Josephus, Flavius. *The Works of Josephus*. Translated by William Whiston. Peabody MA: Hendrickson Publishers, 1987.

Kasher, Rimon. "Scripture in Rabbinic Literature." In *Mikra: Text, Translation, Reading and Interpretation of the Hebrew Bible in Ancient Judaism and Early Christianity*, edited by Martin Jan Mulder, 547-94. Philadelphia: Fortress Press, 1988.

Kautzsch, Emil, editor. *Gesenius' Hebrew Grammar*. Second English edition. Translated by A. E. Cowley. Oxford: Clarendon Press, 1910.

Kemp, Barry J. "Old Kingdom, Middle Kingdom, and Second Intermediate Period." In *Ancient Egypt: A Social History*, edited by B. G. Trigger, B. J. Kemp, D. O'Connor, and A. B. Lloyd, 71-182. Cambridge: Cambridge University Press, 1983.

Kennicott, Benjamin, editor. *Vetus Testamentum Hebraicum cum Variis Lectionibus.* Tomus Primus. Oxford: Clarendon, 1776.

Kirkpatrick, A. F. *The Book of Psalms.* Cambridge Bible for Schools and Colleges. Cambridge: Cambridge University Press, 1902.

Kittel, Bonnie. "Brevard Childs' Development of the Canonical Approach." *Journal for the Study of the Old Testament* 16 (1980): 2-11.

Koch, Klaus, "Der Psalter und seine Redaktionsgeschichte." In *Neue Wege der Psalmenforschung: für Walter Beyerlin,* edited by Klaus Seybold and Erich Zenger, 243-77. Freiburg: Herder, 1994.

Kraus, H.-J. *Psalms 1–59. A Commentary* and *Psalms 60–150. A Commentary.* Translated by H. C. Oswald. Minneapolis: Augsburg Publishing House, 1988 and 1989.

Kselman, John S. "Psalm 146 in Its Context." *Catholic Biblical Quarterly* 50 (1988): 587-99.

_____. "Psalm 3: A Structural and Literary Study." *Catholic Biblical Quarterly* 49 (1987): 572-80.

Kugel, James L., and Rowan A. Greer. *Early Biblical Interpretation.* Philadelphia: Westminster Press, 1986.

Lambert, W. G., and Simon B. Parker, editors. *Enuma Elis: The Babylonian Epic of Creation, the Cuneiform Text.* Oxford: Clarendon Press, 1966.

Landes, George. "The Canonical Approach to Introducing the Old Testament: Prodigy and Problems." *Journal for the Study of the Old Testament* 16 (1980): 32-39.

Lichtheim, Miriam. *Ancient Egyptian Literature.* Volume 1. Berkeley: University of California Press, 1973.

MacIntosh, A. A. "A Consideration of the Problems Presented by Psalm II, 11 and 12." *Journal of Theological Studies* 27 (1976): 1-14.

Mays, James Luther. *Psalms.* Interpretation: A Bible Commentary for Teaching and Preaching. Louisville: Westminster/John Knox Press, 1994.

_____. "The David of the Psalms." *Interpretation* 40 (1986): 143-55.

_____. *The Lord Reigns: A Theological Handbook to the Psalms.* Louisville: Westminster/John Knox Press, 1994.

_____. "The Place of the Torah-Psalms in the Psalter." *Journal of Biblical Literature* 106 (1987): 3-12.

McCann, J. Clinton, Jr. "Psalm 73: A Microcosm of Old Testament Theology." In *The Listening Heart: Essays in Wisdom and the Psalms in Honor of Roland E. Murphy, O. Carm.,* edited by K. Hoglund et al., 247-57. Sheffield UK: JSOT Press, 1987.

_____, editor. *The Shape and Shaping of the Psalter.* Journal for the Study of the Old Testament Supplement Series 159. Sheffield UK: Sheffield Academic Press, 1993.

_____. *A Theological Introduction to the Book of Psalms: The Psalms as Torah.* Nashville: Abingdon Press, 1993.

_____, and Beth Tanner. "Moses, Psalm 90 and the Shape of the Psalter." Unpublished paper presented to the Book of Psalms Group at the Society of Biblical Literature Annual Meeting in San Francisco, 22 November 1992.

Michalowski, Piotr. *The Lamentation Over the Destruction of Sumer and Ur.* Winona Lake IN: Eisenbrauns, 1989.

Millard, Matthias. *Die Komposition des Psalters: ein formgeschichtlicher Ansatz.* Forschungen zum Alten Testament 9. Tübingen: Mohr-Siebeck, 1994.

Miller, J. Maxwell, and John H. Hayes. *A History of Ancient Israel and Judah.* Philadelphia: Westminster Press, 1986.

Morgan, Donn F. *Between Text and Community: The "Writings" in Canonical Interpretation.* Minneapolis: Fortress Press, 1990.

Morkholm, Otto. "Antiochus IV." In *The Cambridge History of Judaism,* volume 2, edited by W. D. Davies and Louis Finkelstein, 278-91. Cambridge: Cambridge University Press, 1989.

Mowinckel, Sigmund. *Psalmen Studien.* Two volumes. Oslo: Skrifter utgitt av Det Norske Videnskaps-Akademi i Olso, 1921–1924; repr.: Amsterdam: Verlag P. Schippers, 1961.

_____. *The Psalms in Israel's Worship.* Two volumes. Translated by D. R. Ap-Thomas. Nashville: Abingdon Press, 1962.

Murphy, Roland E. *The Tree of Life: An Exploration of Biblical Wisdom Literature.* Anchor Bible Reference Library. New York: Doubleday, 1990.

Nasuti, Harry P. *Tradition History and the Psalms of Asaph.* Society of Biblical Literature Dissertation Series 88. Atlanta: Scholars Press, 1988.

Negoită, A. הָגָה *hāghāh.* In *Theological Dictionary of the Old Testament,* volume 3, edited by G. Johannes Botterweck and Helmer Ringgren, translated by John T. Willis, Geoffrey W. Bromiley, and David E. Green, 321-24. Grand Rapids MI: Williams B. Eerdmans Publishing Co., 1978.

Neusner, Jacob. *First Century Judaism in Crisis.* Nashville: Abingdon Press, 1975.

_____. *Judaism in the Beginning of Christianity.* Philadelphia: Fortress Press, 1984.

_____. *The Mishnah: A New Translation.* New Haven: Yale University Press, 1988.

_____. *Self-Fulfilling Prophecy: Exile and Return in the History of Judaism.* Atlanta: Scholars Press, 1990.

Noth, Martin. *The History of Israel.* Second edition. London: A. & C. Black; New York: Harper & Bros., 1960.

Polzin, Robert. "'The Ancestress in Danger' in Danger." *Semeia* 3 (1975): 81-97.

Pritchard, James B., editor. *Ancient Near Eastern Texts Relating to the Old Testament*. Third edition. Princeton: Princeton University Press, 1969.

Rainey, Anson F. "Further Remarks on the Hebrew Verbal System." *Hebrew Studies* 29 (1988): 35-42.

_____. "The Ancient Prefix Conjugation in the Light of Amarnah Canaanite." *Hebrew Studies* 27 (1986): 4-19.

Reindl, J. "Weisheitliche Bearbeitung von Psalmen: Ein Beitrag zum Verständnis der Sammlung des Psalters." In *Congress Volume: Vienna 1980*, edited by J. A. Emerton, 338-39. Leiden: E. J. Brill, 1981.

Robinson, A. "Deliberate but Misguided Haplography Explains Psalm 2:11-12." *Zeitschrift für die alttestamentliche Wissenschaft* 89 (1977): 421-22.

Ross, J.F. "Psalm 73." In *Israelite Wisdom: Theological and Literary Essays in Honor of Samuel Terrien*, edited by J. G. Gammie et al., 161-75. Missoula MT: Scholars Press, 1978.

Sanders, E. P. *Judaism: Practice and Belief: 63 B.C.E.–66 C.E.* Philadelphia: Trinity Press International, 1992.

Sanders, James A. *Canon and Community: A Guide to Canonical Criticism*. Guides to Biblical Scholarship. Philadelphia: Fortress Press, 1984.

_____. *The Dead Sea Psalms Scroll*. Ithaca NY: Cornell University Press, 1967.

_____. *From Sacred Story to Sacred Text*. Philadelphia: Fortress Press, 1987.

_____. *Torah and Canon*. Philadelphia: Fortress Press, 1972.

Sarna, Nahum M. "Book of Psalms." In *Encyclopaedia Judaica*, volume 13, edited by Cecil Roth, 1303-34. Jerusalem: Keter Publishing House, 1971.

Schäfer, Peter. "The Hellenistic and Maccabaean Periods." In *Israelite and Judaean History*, edited by John H. Hayes and J. Maxwell Miller, 539-604. London: SCM Press, 1977.

Schökel, Luis Alonso. "The Poetic Structure of Psalm 42-43." *Journal for the Study of the Old Testament* 1 (1976): 4-21.

Soggin, J. Alberto. *A History of Israel: From the Beginnings to the Bar Kochba Revolt, A.D. 135*. London: SCM Press, 1984.

Sundberg, A. C. "The 'Old Testament': A Christian Canon." *Catholic Biblical Quarterly* 30 (1968): 143-55.

Tate, Marvin E. *Psalms 51–100*. Word Biblical Commentary 20. Dallas: Word Books, 1990.

Trigger, B. G. "The Rise of Egyptian Civilization." In *Ancient Egypt: A Social History*, edited by B. G. Trigger, B. J. Kemp, D. O'Connor, and A. B. Lloyd, 1-70. Cambridge: Cambridge University Press, 1983.

van der Toorn, K. "Ordeal Procedures in the Psalms and the Passover Meal." *Vetus Testamentum* 38 (1988): 427-45.

Vawter, Bruce. "Postexilic Prayer and Hope." *Catholic Biblical Quarterly* 37 (1975): 460-70.

von Rad, Gerhard. *God at Work in Israel.* Translated by John H. Marks. Nashville: Abingdon Press, 1980.

Waltke, Bruce K. "Superscripts, Postscripts, or Both." *Journal of Biblical Literaure* 110 (1991): 583-96.

Watts, J. D. W. "Psalm 2 in the Context of Biblical Theology." *Horizons in Biblical Theology* 12 (1990): 73-91.

Wellhausen, Julius. *The Book of Psalms.* Polychrome Bible. London: James Clark, 1889.

Westermann, Claus. *The Praise of God in the Psalms.* Translated by Keith R. Crim. Richmond VA: John Knox Press, 1965.

_____. *Praise and Lament in the Psalms.* Translated by Keith R. Crim and Richard N. Soulen. Atlanta: John Knox Press, 1981.

Whitelam, Keith W. "Israelite Kingship. The Royal Ideology and Its Opponents." In *The World of Ancient Israel.* Edited by R. E. Clements. Cambridge: Cambridge University Press, 1989.

Willis, John T. "Psalm 1—An Entity." *Zeitschrift für die alttestamentliche Wissenschaft* 91 (1979): 381-401.

Wilson, Gerald H. "A First Century CE Date for the Closing of the Hebrew Psalter?" In *Haim M. I. Gevaryahu Memorial Volume,* edited by Joshua J. Adler, 136-43. Jerusalem: World Jewish Bible Center, 1990.

_____. *The Editing of the Hebrew Psalter.* Society of Biblical Literature Dissertation Series 76. Edited by J. J. M. Roberts. Chico CA: Scholars Press, 1985.

_____. "The Use of Royal Psalms at the 'Seams' of the Hebrew Psalter." *Journal for the Study of the Old Testament* 35 (1986): 85-94.

_____. "The Use of 'Untitled' Psalms in the Hebrew Psalter." *Zeitschrift für die alttestamentliche Wissenschaft* 97 (1985): 404-13.

Zevit, Ziony. "On Talking Funny in Biblical Henglish and Solving a Problem of the YAQTUL Past Tense." *Hebrew Studies* 29 (1988): 25-33.

Indexes

Author Index

Scripture Index

(References are to Hebrew [MT] versification.)

Ancient Sources Index

Subject Index

Hebrew Word Index

CPSIA information can be obtained at www.ICGtesting.com
Printed in the USA
LVOW041441240912

300097LV00004B/75/A